What others are saying about this book:

This book doesn't waste your time on abstract theories that have no relevance in the real world. The author uses real life examples, thought-provoking quotes and specific suggestions to show readers how they can acquire the communication skills, clout and impact so they can lead gracefully and get the respect they deserve.
— CHRISTINE MCALISTER, BUSINESS OWNER - SCRIBES

I finally get it. I knew there were differences, now I can enjoy the methods and approaches I use, stop worrying and get the job done, my way!
— CINDY BOSA, MANAGER, ACCOUNTING EXPRESS

The Velvet Hammer has given me insight into every challenge I've faced in running my business. This book also helped me understand myself better—I can now manage in a way that feels more natural AND WORKS!
— DAWN CARTWRIGHT, MANAGER - 6TH FLOOR PREPRESS

The majority of people
leave because of poor leadership...
Be the one they stay for.

THE *Velvet* Hammer

PowHERful Leadership Lessons for Women Who Don't Golf

Elaine Allison

positive presentations plus inc.

Vancouver, British Columbia, Canada

The Velvet Hammer
PowHERful Leadership Lessons for Women Who Don't Golf
by Elaine Allison

Copyright ©2006 by Elaine Allison
First Edition 2006

Published by
Positive Presentations Plus Inc.
2241 Stafford Ave.
Port Coquitlam, BC V3C 4X5
Orders@thevelvethammer.com
www.thevelvethammer.com

ISBN-13: 978-0-9739065-0-9
ISBN-10: 0-9739065-0-2

Library and Archives Canada Cataloguing in Publication
Allison, Elaine, 1959-
        The velvet hammer : powHERful [sic] leadership lessons for women who don't golf / Elaine Allison.
Includes index.
ISBN 0-9739065-0-2
        1. Leadership in women. 2. Leadership. 3. Women executives. I. Title.
HD6054.3.A45 2006   658.4'092'082
C2005-906482-X

Unattributed quotations are by Elaine Allison
Published in Canada
Text Design: Dotti Albertine

Dedication

*For my daughter, Nicole
and all the other daughters
who've come before us and
will come after us
who want to lead!*

CONTENTS

CONTENTS

FOREWORD

There are two groups of people; those who believe in learning throughout their lifetime, and then everybody else. I refer to the first group as being on the "train of continuous learning."

Everybody who is on the train of continuous learning has the potential to be a great leader. In order to increase your chances of being a successful leader, you need four key ingredients, which include:

- willingness to "take charge"
- knowledge in your industry, field or organization
- knowledge of effective leadership
- support from a mentor or a sponsor

When you believe in continuous learning, you create the environment and the opportunities for you to learn and improve your leadership every day. Access to the skills can be daunting and expensive. This book is not only an effective way to get access to the skills from a compelling leadership educator but the skills set out in the book are all from a woman's point of view, something I have found challenging to find—or not readily available.

Leaders come in all varieties and exist at all levels of an organization, both with the title of leader and informal leaders. Sometimes, the best training ground for leadership is in the volunteer sector. Don't think for a moment that the rules for leadership don't apply in an unpaid position! In fact, it is actually much harder to mobilize volunteers to follow your lead. Leadership accomplishments in your volunteer work can be directly applicable to paid positions.

This book provides excellent tips and practical examples that will increase your knowledge about effective leadership and is distinctly applicable to women. Elaine illustrates the "how you can do it" concept with memorable stories presenting truths about how to become stronger, better and more effective in your role as a leader, manager or supervisor. You can apply these concepts starting today!

Developing leadership abilities and assuming leadership roles will allow you to become all you can be. Let your enthusiasm build and your potential unfold as you read this book and discover how easy it can be.

> "Some are born great, some achieve greatness, and some have greatness thrust upon them."
> —TWELFTH NIGHT, ACT II, SC. 5

To paraphrase Shakespeare: Women are born leaders, some achieve leadership (according to plan) and some have leadership thrust upon them. Let's be prepared to be great leaders!

— D.W. CAMPBELL, P. ENG., Founder and President —amonavi consulting group inc., National President (2004-06), BPW Canada— The Canadian Federation of Business and Professional Women's Clubs—The voice of working women since 1930

ACKNOWLEDGMENTS

Since I was ten, I wanted to write a book. I just didn't know then that it would be a business book or that I would become so passionate about helping people succeed. My childhood babysitter, Michelle Hollis, at my high school reunion some twenty years ago asked me if I'd written my book yet. I looked at her in disbelief. "How did you know my secret?" I asked. She said, "You used to be in your room writing thirty-page stories instead of watching television." So I thank her for re-planting the seed that day.

As I moved forward with the writing of this book, you can imagine the fold of people that have been brought in to ensure it got completed. I need to say thank you firstly to my husband Dave, who has encouraged and supported me, every step along the way. My children Michael and Nicole and step-children Tamara and Corey who teach and inspire me every day. My father who taught me, "When the going gets tough, the tough get going," and my mother (who I think of every day), who helped me soften my edges.

Whether it is a full read, a partial look over, coaching or encouragement, you need it all just to keep going. They are as follows; Dotti Albertine, Sandy & Terry Allison, Kim Anderson, Ingrid Bredin, Cheryl Cran,

ACKNOWLEDGMENTS

Darla D.W. Campbell, Dawn Cartwright, Barbara Harkness, Sam Horn, Roberta Kelly, Jan B. King, Christine Legg, Jill Lublin, Christine McAllister, Cathy Osborne, Dan Poynter, Dr. Brad McRae, The Robb family, Doug Stevenson, Susan Sweeney and "The Bunch Broads"—Laura, Georgia, Dianne, Linda and Rita who have been my "ya-yas" throughout my life.

INTRODUCTION

WHY READ THIS BOOK?

Do you wonder if there are differences when managing people as a woman vs. your male counterparts? Did you know it is actually science that makes it different? Would you like to know some of the best techniques that great women leaders use to guide and direct—and get things done? Would you like to be respected and admired by both men and women, even when there are tough decisions to be made? Can you see where the team can go, but feel you need new insights on how to take them there? Are you hitting barriers and obstacles that you feel might be holding you back?

This book investigates the many challenges women in management, supervisory or leadership roles encounter and then offers concrete steps and ideas—which you can incorporate today—to overcoming those challenges. This book is not filled with abstract theories—but gives real life examples and strategies for women managing others. I've dubbed them *Velvet Hammer* techniques. If you are ready to become a Velvet Hammer and lead with grace and eloquence, get listened to, and make the difference and impact you know you can—then this book is for you.

CHAPTER 1

If You Want Breakfast,
Get Up and Get Dressed

CELEBRATING THE DIFFERENCES

MY JOURNEY BEGINS

A Velvet Hammer: A woman who manages with
grace and eloquence and still gets things done!

AS I walked across the parking lot, the snow squeaked under my boots. It was my third day on the job as one of Canada's first female prison guards in an all-male maximum security prison. I was 19 years old. My job description said that I was responsible for "the care and supervision of male maximum security incarcerates." I had never led or supervised anyone in my life; I'd had no supervisory or leadership training (which I later found out in my research is typical for many stepping into a supervisory or managerial role).

I had gone to college in order to work with children in trouble with the law, but my course was under the auspices of the Ministry of Correctional Services, which had recently transferred the responsibility for children to the Ministry of Social Services. I was asked at what prison I wanted to do my student placement. I didn't have a car to get to the female facility, so here I was getting off the bus in front of the newest maximum security holding center for men.

I still remember the day I learned my first leadership lesson, of how women would be impacted in this role and what we could do about it. It was my turn to go into the unit and serve breakfast to the inmates. Forty men waited for the wagon to be wheeled in for their first meal of the day. The stench was foul, mostly because of the stale smoke from *Daily Mail* roll-your-own cigarettes. Residents only got a change of clothing and bedding once a week. For the past two days, the male officer who had been assigned to supervise me had carefully demonstrated how spoons were given to inmates one at a time and then carefully counted when the trays came back, to ensure they were not made into weapons. Easy enough, I thought.

He had not prepared me, however, for what was about to happen to me—it had not happened to him. As I opened each cell door, the inmates popped out of their cells wearing only their boxer shorts, or worse—naked. Not even my brother or my father had ever done this in front of me. The inmates were smirking amongst themselves. Even the officer at the door who was supposed to be my backup was smirking. I was humiliated. I went home that evening, acutely aware of the differences, and vowed to find something that was going to work for me— a woman in 'their' world. Little did I know that this early lesson would become the premise of my book.

The next day I went into the unit. I kicked on each cell door and stated, "If you want breakfast, get up and get dressed." One by one, each inmate did exactly what I had asked. As I did not have the strength, size or physical authority to be able to enforce what I wanted, the first leadership lesson I learned that day was "Set out your expectations upfront," without too many details, apologies or explanations.

Velvet Hammer Technique #1
SET EXPECTATIONS UP FRONT.

Respect is earned; it is not automatically deserved because you've been given a title. As a woman, some days I feel I have had to work harder, but now I feel I just had to work smarter and figure things out situation by situation. Often I would beat myself up because what worked for a man didn't work for me, and I felt incompetent. Too often it was a male who pointed out my failures to me. Often when I encountered difficult situations, I tried something I'd read in a book, written by a male, on how to set a vision and gain focus. I found I couldn't focus enough, as I multi-tasked my way through the day and was left feeling scattered.

Little did I know that my instinctive reactions were really the advantages of being a female leader, and I soon learned not to allow someone else's perspective to discourage me from doing what was working for me. I did, however, look at what wasn't working, and had the ability to adapt where necessary. I also studied gender differences and instead of getting mad at my male counterparts, I began to appreciate why and how they did things, and what they did, and I learned to bring their talents to the table. I'm hoping to share my insights with you in this book. Feel free to experiment in order to determine which strategies work best for you.

QUALIFYING GENERALIZATIONS

I want to explain my approach up front. When I speak in generalizations, such as "men normally do this, or women typically do that," keep in mind that not 100% of people fit either gender pattern. It is like speaking generally about other cultures or the habits of other countries. You may hear that in Japan people bow, but when I traveled there not *everyone* bowed; it is an example of a broad generalization. I am expressing my opinion and my observations only—there will always be exceptions to every rule.

Velvet Hammer Technique #2
DON'T GET ANGRY AT GENDER DIFFERENCES—
LEARN TO UNDERSTAND AND EMBRACE THEM!

Let me share with you some of my research and identify why men and women often feel confused by one another. As I read through stacks of books I was relieved to discover that the differences were real. For many years, I tried to be equal to men and just like them. This, however, is truly an impossible dream, and for many reasons neither gender should want to be like the other, as it just doesn't work. People have different expectations of women and men and this is a simple reality.

The wonderful thing about acknowledging the differences between the way men and women lead is that now we know that the frustrations we may have felt are based on scientific fact, not something we are making up in our heads. The differences are real. These differences come from biological variables such as hormones and brain structure, plus cultural differences and even evolution. Once I understood this, I could laugh at myself, use my greatest assets to their greatest advantage, and embrace the men in my life and their ways, methods and conduct. It is not that I am overly emotional, flighty, disorganized, too detail-oriented, or that I care too much. Nor should men be criticized for their perceived flaws. We are just completely different on many levels.

THE DIFFERENCES

The differences between men and women in leadership roles can be attributed to several factors; evolution, hormones, brains and cultural expectations. As the book progresses, you will note subtle references to these differences throughout each chapter.

EVOLUTION

The first difference between men and women that we'll discuss comes from evolution. If you look at historical evidence, the men were hunters (the ancestral version of bringing home the bacon), and needed to be both competitive and aggressive to accomplish this. Their power came from these traits. Today in the workplace, it is generally accepted by many men and women that men can often 'command' power and respect. This works quite well for men and they often get things done, and traditionally we've been more accepting of this behavior from men. On the other hand, if a woman 'commands,' she is too often perceived as a 'bitch' and may alienate the very people she depends upon to get things done.

Women through the ages have been hard-wired to nurture, stay home, gather, run the household and raise the young. Women traditionally shared duties using the resources of the village to keep family life running. Women value inclusiveness. Using inclusiveness in their vision of managing is a wonderful way to get things done. This need for inclusiveness prevents us from using the most direct approach in certain situations, as we try to keep the village intact. This can sometimes make us 'velvety,' and we do not always accomplish our goals as we try to get everyone to collaborate. It is a wonderful trait and works very well in some leadership situations; however it may need to be modified. We need to recognize when to step in and make the tough decisions, which are sometimes hasty and sometimes unpopular. We often don't want to exclude anyone, but a good leader knows they cannot always be liked or keep everyone happy;

their job is to ensure that people are productive. In Chapter 8, I will offer you a script for a direct approach to correcting performance issues that I find works amazingly well for women, but does not alienate the person, even when you are trying to correct their behavior or conduct.

OUR NEED TO NURTURE
CREATES A BALANCING ACT

The need to nurture is a wonderful trait to embrace. However, it can work for and against us. Can you see how this tendency may create stress for us? What if you are not at home looking after things because you are looking after things in your leadership role? The struggle and guilt begins. I know this, as I've always had a busy, full life, quite often involving travel. The other mothers often look at me with raised eyebrows, as I fly in a few minutes late for the recital, and the guilt begins. But this nurturing trait—and its associated guilt—is also an advantage for us, as it keeps us centered and balanced. Who'd want to spend that much time at the office anyway?

Keeping a healthy balance between our careers and the rest of our lives requires the delegation techniques discussed in Chapter 4. Delegation allows us to control the outflow of duties, tasks and responsibilities that need to be fulfilled, but not always by us. We simply need more of an infrastructure to accomplish everything in the various arenas of our life, and I believe it will be women who put things into place in our corporations, governments and associations, when creative solutions are sought.

TESTOSTERONE

It is well recognized that men have more testosterone, a male sex hormone, in their systems than women. This hormone aids in meeting the historical requirement for aggressiveness and competitiveness (the fight or flight response). You can see why men get the promotions; they are used to stepping up and competing, often coming forward to be seen as the biggest and the best in order to survive.

Could this truly be hormonal? Are women gentler by nature and just being patient, hoping someone will recognize their talents? Men often have a desire to win, and will draw their superior's attention to why they should get the promotion—and they'll often take the steps to prove it. Could it be that when a male boss promotes a man rather than a woman, even when they both have the exact same qualifications, it is because the boss feels more familiar with or prefers the methods used by men? It is what men know. Maybe it is not discrimination at all, but they just feel more comfortable with the way their male counterpart approaches things.

Also, do women truly get bogged down with the details, making things look more complicated than they are? Maybe becoming more competitive and tenacious is the appropriate advice for some women. It may help. Ask yourself, am I being held back, does the glass ceiling really exist, or am I allowing it to exist in my head? I wonder if this is why, as women pass through menopause and lose estrogen levels and therefore increase the testosterone in their systems, they often move ahead, move forward or move on in their lives, and do more for themselves rather than everyone else.

ESTROGEN, PROGESTERONE

Testosterone isn't the only hormone affecting human behavior in the workplace. The fluctuating female hormones estrogen and progesterone not only play monthly havoc with our feelings, moods and emotions, they can actually define us. Estrogen and progesterone aid our ability to nurture and allow us to create a village-like atmosphere in our organizations. High levels of estrogen provide the strong nesting urges (belonging) and nurturing feelings rooted in caring for others. Estrogen also helps curb testosterone levels in a woman. Progesterone, another female hormone, causes caring or nurturing feelings, which may explain our acute need for inclusiveness.

OXYTOCIN VS. ADRENALINE

Oxytocin is another female hormone. High levels are secreted during birth and labor and also—believe it or not!—when women are under stress. Men produce higher levels of adrenaline when under stress (once again another fight or flight response hormone) than women do; although we produce some adrenaline, we actually produce higher levels of oxytocin. If women don't secrete as much adrenaline under stress as once was thought, does this explain why women have a high need for personal interaction when they are stressed? When a crisis hits, oxytocin makes us feel, "Oh we should call a meeting." We often just want to "talk it over," bond, and befriend, just to put things into perspective. "We have to talk" is a common phrase in my household when I'm stressed, and *now I know it might be my oxytocin*. Men might be sitting in the meeting thinking, "Just make a decision," as their adrenaline (fight or flight hormone) can be telling them to "fix it" or "leave it alone."

Women often don't want action or a solution—at least, not immediately—they often just want to interact and talk it through. They reach a solution using an alternative route. Can you see how this might look foolish in a boardroom full of men? They want to do something about it to get results, and women want to talk it over to find results. Men may be asking, "How is that going to get results?" and may be thinking, "Can you get to the point or make a decision?"

Now that we are out of the industrial era, there is no longer the same need for hierarchical structures and outdated leadership styles (and their subsequent power over employees). Women's hormones can now work for us in an unprecedented positive way. The new leadership style in today's global economy requires collaboration, coordination, empowerment and the sharing of power and information. It truly does take a village to get things done; both men and women can bring great things to the table. When men and women understand how hormones affect them, it may become more acceptable for us to conduct ourselves using our own natural tendencies.

Also, later in life as women's testosterone levels rise and estrogen levels decrease, they may actually become more competitive and seize additional opportunities to take risks (this is often combined with other changes in personal situations, such as greater financial security and children leaving the home). One must be aware, however, that not taking risks earlier in life does not always benefit us. Give this idea careful thought, considering the balancing act typical of the earlier stages in a woman's life. I turned down one management job when I was pregnant with my second child and felt the timing was just not right. I am still not sure to this day if it was the right decision. With such a wonderful support system at home, I believe I would have been fine.

THE BRAIN—WOMEN USE BOTH SIDES SIMULTANEOUSLY

If hormones weren't enough, you should see what our brains are doing to behavior in the workplace. We can see the differences in brain functions by using MRIs and PET scans while men and women are doing various tasks. For instance, when doing a series of tasks: in men's brains only one hemisphere lights up, while in women both hemispheres light up. Brain scans have shown time and time again that men favor the right hemisphere and use the right hemisphere more efficiently than women, hence an aptitude for math and spatial acuity. This allows men to be localized, focused and specialized (single task). Women can sometimes make the assumption that men appear single-minded on an issue and men can perceive women (master multi-taskers) using both hemispheres as scattered. I know, our multi-tasking gift allows us to get a lot done, something most workplaces appreciate from their administrative employees.

Men generally score higher in things such as math aptitude and spatial acuity. Women can score well on the computation component, but not always as well on the aptitude and critical thinking skills (like engineering). For example, try programming a VCR. The men I know seem to be able to open directions and program the VCR on the first try. Men have a tendency to work on singular tasks and can excel at being focused. Women seem to have the unique ability to take it all in, including all the details, so if both sides of the brain are working simultaneously no wonder we can look after what some might call 'the small stuff' (it is not that small when you add it all up, though). Think of a religious holiday, like those who celebrate Christmas. My husband will typically get the lights and a tree up, and I typically do all the rest; the gift buying, the extravagant meals, baking and treats, all the while trimming the tree, decorating the house, with music playing in the background and the log in the fireplace and even those scented candles. It truly isn't finished until everything is in its place. If something is missed, I often take the blame (ever forget the cranberry sauce?).

If women do use both sides of the brain simultaneously, and can multi-task efficiently, we often struggle to see why a man can't do the same. We can appear to be scattered and disorganized, but somehow we also seem to get a lot done. When we do take too much on, however, we become overwhelmed and sometimes resentful (the brain can only take in so much data). See Chapter 9 on 'Don't Get It All Done—Get Help' and find out how to celebrate this talent, enjoy our busy and full lives and learn how to balance it all.

Another difference in brain structure is the fact that women have larger dendrites (tube like connections) running between both hemispheres. The larger dendrites may explain why women have the ability not only to multi-task, but to see things from a holistic viewpoint, a feature sometimes known as *women's intuition*. We have the ability to pull together details from all the senses, including any emotional overtones. When asked to prove something, often women can't articulate why—they know because they can just *sense* it. This ability to use our inner guidance can be a real gift for women. Women tend to be able to read people's feelings, sense what is going on and look at things holistically, worrying about how their decisions affect their team, families, the environment, and anyone or anything else that might not be taken care of.

We even differ in our focuses—women speak mostly of the people in their lives, while men speak about sports, politics and news. Just look at the magazine articles in certain publications, or differences in internet use between men and women. When you are in a meeting with men, expect the conversation to change and try to keep up with the daily reports in the paper and news from time to time, if you want to break into their conversation. Start talking about your parents or best friend, and they may move away. I believe this is why at gatherings, functions, meetings and so forth you often see the women collecting in one area and the men in the other.

Velvet Hammers—women who lead with grace and eloquence—understand and honor these differences. The differences are scientific and not excuses. Velvet Hammers have always known instinctively that we could not just put on shoulder pads and play golf, as well as all the other great ideas we've tried, just to fit in.

When it comes to leadership, women are making a mark and a difference. Their contributions are significant and everyone benefits from them. This is not a protest book, but a book of celebration. With each of the leadership skills in the forthcoming chapters I've tried to convey my twist on things and offer you a woman's perspective. I've dubbed them Velvet Hammer techniques so that when situations crop up, you've got some strategies in your back pocket. I've also tried to give you real life examples that have worked for me, with men or women, and that you can take into your area. My hope is that you will honor your inherent behaviors and abilities, adapt where you can and need to, as well as be able to make your mark and make a difference.

Velvet Hammer Technique #3
CELEBRATE YOUR INHERENT FEMALE TRAITS AND UTILIZE THEM TO THEIR FULLEST WHERE THEY AID YOU. ADAPT ONLY WHEN NECESSARY.

All assessments, checklists, worksheets and evaluations found in this book are available at:

www.thevelvethammer.com

Download your copies today!

CHAPTER 2

In a Meeting—Shut Up!

ASSESSING YOURSELF AS A LEADER

HUMILITY & GRACE

You are never truly a leader until your team is ready to follow.

I was 29 years old when I started in my first management position. It was with a major international charter airline, and it was unionized. I was to manage 30 flight attendants administratively from an office (conduct annual performance reviews, keep track of attendance and tardiness, customer complaints, etc., while doing two office days a month), as well as manage flights on board a Boeing 747 and other large aircrafts with about 15 crew members, 17 days a month. Most of the staff members were senior to me in both experience and age.

The training I received was mostly technical—how to write performance reviews; fill out paperwork regarding duty-free customs, safety, and other documents; manage crew assignments and briefings; handle any scheduling changes or issues overseas, etc. This was supplemented by leadership training on how to enforce discipline and create an outline of the important points of the contract agreement. I remember my father saying to me, "How are you going to manage these people, you haven't ever managed before, nor taken a course. Are you sure you know what you are getting yourself into?"

I did not know what he meant; I thought I was well-prepared, as I'd been a flight attendant for two years, and I already knew how to do the job. How hard could it be? If you've ever been in this situation, you may have felt that "nothing" could have prepared you for this! The leadership skills needed to lead and direct and still get things done are diverse and expansive and you often don't come to the table with every skill intact. I wish I'd had a checklist or roadmap of what I was going to need to learn. My wish is that you can benefit from my experience using the Velvet Hammer techniques, and through the examples and points illustrated.

ASSESSMENTS – EVALUATING STRENGTHS, WEAKNESSES AND SKILL GAPS

The following assessments are going to help you identify your strengths and weaknesses and your skill gaps and show you how to make the most of your natural abilities. First, we are going to explore where you are in your leadership skills in general. Secondly, we will assess how well your female tendencies in a leadership role serve you in male-dominated situations (they are all repeated questions from women in my seminars), and identify areas where you might want to adapt. Finally, we will profile 'your' personality and offer you ideas on your primary or preferred behaviors and how to manage your opposite style—the person who may be driving you crazy.

This profile is more in-depth than mere gender differences. It will give you insight into who 'you' are in different interactions and can provide insights into how to adapt when working with another personality. It was something I learned years ago and I found it one of the most significant lessons to understand human behavior and not get angry with people. It also taught me that in one arena these attributes can be my greatest strength, but in another arena, those exact same traits can be my worst enemy.

Personality profiling is common in the business environment and you may be familiar with the tools available. I've tried to simplify it so you get the general idea. For further information on personality profiling, I recommend testing programs that are available on the Internet or see the appendix for a list of sources. So get your pen ready and then we'll score your results. After each assessment, I've offered some summaries for you to ponder.

DETERMINING YOUR SKILL GAPS IN LEADERSHIP

RATE YOURSELF: Please rate yourself from 1 to 4 in each of the following areas.

1 = not descriptive of me at all
2 = descriptive of me once in a while
3 = often descriptive of me
4 = always descriptive of me

___ 1. I have clear goals for my team that are measurable and understood.

___ 2. I set an example for my team based on what I expect from them (on time, meet deadlines, follow through on commitments, etc.).

___ 3. I handle change and new situations calmly.

___ 4. When a team member is upset with me, I try to correct it by listening to his or her ideas.

___ 5. I am available for questions, offer ideas and support my team on a regular and ongoing basis.

___ 6. I use a tracking system to monitor results and deadlines.

___ 7. I know how to arrange a budget, work within the budget and handle overruns.

___ 8. I can address issues with people, without hesitation, embarrassment or aggression.

___ 9. The people I direct are extremely motivated and continually contribute.

___10. I handle conflict with ease, and aggressive behavior does not intimidate me.

___11. When I get overwhelmed, I build an action plan.

___12. I recognize the contribution each team member can or cannot make and have the ability to direct them accordingly.

A score of 4 indicates mastery in this area.

A score of 3 means you are most likely meeting the expectations of your team in that area.

A score of 2 indicates a need for improvement in that area. Obtain further training if you don't feel this book gives you enough strategies to improve in this area.

A score of 1 indicates a skill gap.

A lower end score in any of these areas indicates that further learning may be required in that particular area. Please review each of the chapters to determine if a technique discussed in the book will assist you. Also, further training may be required in any of these areas you feel you struggle with. See appendices for a list of public seminar companies, both national and international.

Photocopy these pages.
Or visit www.thevelvethammer.com
to download the evaluation.

The next exercise is one that you can give to your team and let them evaluate you. This is called 360° feedback. What they tell you can represent some of the most useful feedback you will obtain. To encourage honesty, ensure that all feedback is anonymous. The results will help you determine if your evaluation is supported by that of your team. Remember the intent of the team survey is to help identify areas that you can improve and learn from. If a team is disgruntled with your style or the techniques you use, they probably won't perform well. Take the responses seriously, not personally; again a low score may just indicate a skill gap that you can seek skills to help.

To be completed by your team:

**MANAGER'S TEAM APPRAISAL FORM
(360° FEEDBACK)**

Please rate your leader, supervisor or manager from 1 to 4 in each of the following areas.

1 = not descriptive of them at all
2 = descriptive of them once in a while
3 = often descriptive of them
4 = always descriptive of them
NA = not applicable, or have not observed

___ 1. My manager provides clear goals for our team that are measurable and understood.

___ 2. My manager sets an example for the team (on time, meets deadlines, follows through on commitments, etc.).

___ 3. My manager handles change and new situations calmly.

___ 4. When I am upset about an issue, my manager handles it by at least listening to my ideas.

___ 5. My manager is available for questions, offers ideas, and supports me on a regular and ongoing basis.

___ 6. My manager monitors results and deadlines well to manage workflows.

___ 7. My manager is competent with arranging budgets, and can handle overruns.

___ 8. My manager can address issues with people without hesitation, embarrassment or aggression.

___ 9. The people my manager directs often feel motivated to contribute continually.

___10. My manager handles conflict with ease, and aggressive behavior does not seem to intimidate them.

___11. When my manager gets overwhelmed with work, she appears to have an action plan.

___12. My manager recognizes the contribution each team member can or cannot make and has the ability to direct staff accordingly.

Photocopy these pages.
Or visit www.thevelvethammer.com
to download the evaluation.

HELP! WHAT DO I DO WHEN... SCENARIOS (GENDER DIFFERENCE SITUATIONS)

The situations below are typical scenarios that women bring up in my seminars time and time again, requesting "What do I do when... ?" In this quick review, answer the questions honestly. Think about what you have really done or said in these situations, *not what you think is the right answer*. If you have never been exposed to the situation, try the question anyway; if you ever do run into it, you will then have some options.

Scenario 1

You're feeling impatient about a deadline. You need something from a male team member by the end of day. What would you say?

a) Are you finished with that report?

b) Do you need help finishing that report?

c) At what time can I expect the report today?

Scenario 2

When a male team member is pushing you for something that you *don't* want to do, you say:

a) I need more time to consider it.

b) I have considered your request and am not convinced it will work.

c) I appreciate your input; however, we will not be exploring the idea further.

Scenario 3

When a male team member is yelling at you, you:

a) Walk away.

b) Defend yourself.

c) Do nothing.

d) Remain impartial, acknowledge their frustration, do not come to the fight and delay the conversation until you can investigate further.

Scenario 4

You are in a room full of men who are completely ignoring you, like you do not exist. You:

a) Do nothing.

b) Try to break into the group's conversation and add a relevant comment.

c) Move into the group's space slowly, then wait to speak to one person first.

Scenario 5

In your presence, a few men are conversing with each other and making what might be construed as sexual innuendos that are not directed at you, but you feel somewhat uncomfortable. They know you are there. You:

a) Leave the room abruptly in disgust.

b) Excuse yourself from the conversation.

c) Tell them their behavior is unacceptable and asked that they stop immediately.

d) Accept it, do nothing.

e) Do not take it personally, change the conversation to another topic.

Photocopy these pages.
Or visit www.thevelvethammer.com
to download the evaluation.

POSSIBLE SUGGESTIONS OR OPTIONS

Options: Scenario 1

In this situation I hate harping on people, especially men; they can perceive it as nagging. A simple question early in the day with the right tone of voice can imply that you are asking for a committed deadline. By offering to help them upfront, you may make them feel incompetent. By asking what time, they will have a chance to explain first what other obligations or challenges they may have, in order to deliver it on time. If there are good reasons for not meeting the deadline, a good leader then discusses what tasks can be moved to free up time for this report, extends the deadline, or offers assistance, either directly or through others. Asking, "Are you finished?" may imply a lack of trust.

Options: Scenario 2

In this scenario it is often best to acknowledge their ideas, comments or suggestions (validate) and be direct about not moving forward with them. If you state, "Not at this time," or, "I need more time to consider it," (when you know you don't), it will only appear wishy-washy if you don't revisit their idea later on. I find this frustrates men that I have supervised, when they 'just want a decision.' Sometimes our holistic thinking allows us to linger in certain situations.

Options: Scenario 3

When a male is yelling at me, or behaves aggressively, I would strongly recommend holding your ground, acknowledge he is frustrated, upset or concerned, and neither agree nor disagree. I refuse to come to the fight. I don't defend my position at this time, I delay it (unless it is an emergency situation and someone is in immediate danger). I deflect by staying neutral. Physically I either remain still until they are finished ranting, ask them to walk with me to a more isolated area (get them out of public), or recommend they bring it up later. If you read the chapter on conflict, I go into this in great detail. Walking away (or stating, "I don't have to put up with this") can exacerbate the situation. Defending your position always makes the other person immediately wrong—the first step to immediate conflict. Doing nothing at all can demonstrate weakness and may allow the person to continue their aggressiveness.

Options: Scenario 4

In this situation, although uncomfortable because often you do stand out as the only 'one' and by all accounts you are different, this situation does not have to be awkward. As with any group, don't interrupt—it is just bad manners. I often move closer and wait until I'm invited in (most people can't ignore space that is being taken up). Often one person will turn to look at you and you can strike up a conversation with them, often they will move to one side and move you into the group. You'll see children—believe it or not—doing this regularly on the playground as they meet other children. They seem to have a unique talent for getting moved into the group. Doing nothing can make matters worse, and don't pout or leave, as it can enforce a stereotype.

Options: Scenario 5

This is the tricky one. Some organizations may even have policies about this, but if they don't you may be on your own. Handling this situation can depend upon the circumstances, so I will attempt to tackle it by giving a number of options, for different contexts. When I worked in an all-male setting, this type of inappropriate bantering was common.

a) If there is no mean intent behind it, you may want to consider excusing yourself from the conversation or not taking it personally and attempting to change the conversation.

b) If it is malicious or has malicious intent, I let them know that the conversation may be best held outside of the arena in which it is taking place (workplace, meeting, formal setting).

c) If there is one person who is the perpetrator, I will speak with them privately.

d) Worst case scenario: remove yourself from the situation (go get a cup of coffee, water or an errand and come back afterwards). Usually the disapproval on my face when I leave says it all.

e) If it is directed at me and I'm humiliated, I either use a quick quip (a talent), or if one doesn't come to me, I state very matter-of-factly, "That one was unfair, uncalled for, or below the belt."

f) If worst comes to worse and they don't stop, I get help, either from human resources or a lawyer.

g) If it is absolutely intolerable, I leave permanently— yes, I quit. One of the reasons I'm no longer a corrections officer is that I was both physically and verbally abused by another male officer. When his conduct was reported by several female corrections officers he got a three-day suspension 'with pay.' We were all represented by the same union, and both shop stewards were male. If you cannot accept or change it, sometimes you have to remove yourself. Remember this was back in the 1970s, when they were just putting females in non-traditional roles and frankly, I don't think they really knew what to do. Today, with the financial rewards the courts are giving out, I may have retired a lot sooner—but then I wouldn't have had all the stories for this book.

BRINGING OUT THE BEST IN YOURSELF AND OTHERS

Understanding that people have distinctly different personalities, approaches and methods was one of the most critical skills I learned when dealing and communicating with others. Any supervisor, manager or leader who learns this necessary skill is better at building relationships with everyone on their team, even if they are different. Once you can identify the inherent traits of different people, especially of someone who typically drives you crazy (your opposite personality style), you'll have empathy and understanding for the way they work and be able to embrace and direct them to where they can capitalize on those traits for the greatest contribution.

A strong woman leader who understands people at this level can also bring this information to the team and use it to resolve team conflicts. Team conflict is covered in greater detail in Chapter 8. Just remember, as you go through this evaluation there is no 'best' style, and each trait listed in one arena as your greatest asset can be your worst enemy in another arena. For example, you will note from my story in this chapter that my 'enthusiasm' when speaking in front of large groups is a gift, yet in a small meeting when I'm a participant, this can be my worst enemy, as I sometimes cut people off in my excitement for an idea. Have a look at the chart and evaluate yourself in the 'Personality Profiles Test' and then see how each style must be adapted to work better with another.

THE VELVET HAMMER
PERSONALITY PROFILES TEST

In the boxes below, for each section check off those behaviors and characteristics that best describe you in a working environment. The quadrant with the most check marks is your primary or preferred personality/behavior style. Note: you may be a blend of two or more styles. That is okay. By the way, there is no right or wrong, best or worst style. *You may even want to get your team to do this profiling, so you can learn more about each other; then offer your team ideas to work better with each other as well.*

**Photocopy these pages.
Or visit www.thevelvethammer.com
to download the evaluation.**

1	2
___ you like results ___ you meet deadlines ___ you feel great when things are done ___ you can command attention *sometimes you feel...* ___ you've bowled some people over ___ you might have been abrupt ___ you expect too much some days ___Total # of checkmarks	___ you like to interact ___ you are the 'ideas' person ___ you are enthusiastic ___ you feel great when everyone is involved *sometimes you feel...* ___ like you've interrupted (again) ___ you might be too excited ___ scattered and disorganized ___ Total # of checkmarks

3	4
___ you like accuracy ___ you like detail and statistics ___ you can pull data together quickly *sometimes you feel...* ___ you can be picky ___ you take too long to make a decision because you want to make sure it is right ___ you are a perfectionist ___ Total # of checkmarks	___ you are loyal, steadfast, responsible ___ you hate letting people down ___ you enjoy harmony and peace *sometimes you feel...* ___ unheard ___ you delay making a decision because you know not everyone will like it ___ you are wishy-washy on a topic ___ Total # of checkmarks

**Your highest score was in
quadrant # _____ = _____**

**(For your personality style
(see the next section)**

NOTE: If you have an equal amount in each quadrant, review your answers and select the ones that *most* describe you in a work or volunteer situation.

No. 1 THE CHIEF	No. 2 THE ENTHUSIAST
The chief has a natural tendency to lead. **They have an innate need to get things done.**	The enthusiast has a great need to interact. Put them alone in a cubicle and they will feel stifled. **They are the natural ideas people and often are highly creative.**
No. 3 THE PROBLEM SOLVER	No. 4 THE FRIEND
The problem solver has a great need and an innate ability for accuracy. They like to get things right. **If you need something done correctly, ask a problem solver.**	The friend has a great need to get along and to keep things going smoothly. **They won't let you down and are the most loyal of the four styles.**

In all the descriptions of these styles, I have noted the greatest asset of each personality type. In one arena this characteristic remains your greatest asset, but in another arena it can become your worst enemy. Those little arrows between the styles show your opposite personality style. Opposite personality styles are often challenged to get along. Their methods and approaches are often completely different.

Velvet Hammer Technique #4
UNDERSTAND YOUR STYLE AND KNOW IN WHAT ARENAS IT WORKS FOR YOU AND WHERE YOU NEED TO ADAPT.

I learned about my personality from an excruciatingly painful performance review. My boss stated, "We love that you can speak to large groups of people and your enthusiasm really helps sell the ideas and products, but in a meeting, SHUT UP! You look like Arnold Horshack (a character in the 70s TV show *Welcome Back Kotter*, an annoying individual who always put his hand up, interrupted everyone and blurted out whatever thought came into his head)." I was mortified. It took me almost six months of psychotherapy to get over that comment, until one day I decided to take heed of the comment. It was the best lesson about myself I'd ever had. "**In a meeting—shut up!,**" you are annoying everyone on your team! In my excitement and enthusiasm, being the Enthusiast that I am, I'd blurt out things as they came into my head. Now when I go to a meeting, I take a pad of paper. If a thought occurs to me, I write it down and bring it up at the appropriate time on the agenda or after the meeting. This makes a huge difference with the teams I work with. It gives others the chance to say something. Do you have someone on your team like this?

WITH OPPOSITE PERSONALITY STYLES

The Enthusiast with The Problem Solver

So, as you know, I'm an Enthusiast. I love creating and am always noted as the 'ideas' person. As mentioned, however, in a meeting my excitement and enthusiasm can take over. Putting up my hand to express my idea, I have a tendency to cut others off mid-sentence. Many find it annoying, but guess which style hates it the *most*? The Problem Solver! They are often deep thinkers and need a lot of time to fully understand a new idea. I'm jumping up and down, very animated, and they look at me like they're thinking, "What planet are you from?" I'm looking at them thinking, "Are you getting how great this could be?" We typically end up leaving the meeting irked with each other, both frustrated, as our methods for completing a task are COMPLETELY OPPOSITE. Neither method is wrong; they are just different. We might go off to the water cooler and complain about the other person, often to our fellow like-styles, who nod in agreement.

Ways for The Enthusiast to adapt and work better with the Problem Solver

- Slow down, wait your turn to speak. Bring a pad of paper and if a thought pops into your head, write it down and bring it up at the appropriate time, or even after the meeting. *This is especially advisable if you are the leader.*

- Ensure you have an appreciation for all facts and details.
- Be prepared; if you are not 100% sure, explain that you can check again. Don't make a Problem Solver appear to be wrong (they are often right, as their greatest strength is that they've usually done their homework).
- Appreciate that Problem Solvers can help you look good. If they find typos, errors, or point things out to you, thank them—they make you look stronger.
- Remember: their intent is not to get you, but to get it right.

The Problem Solver with The Enthusiast

The Problem Solver is typically fabulous at gathering the necessary facts to back up thoughts and ideas. The need for detail and to get things right is commendable. Time is needed to process information. The Enthusiast will move quickly in their speech and their actions, often driving you crazy. If Enthusiasts do that, request that they put their thoughts into an email, or on paper and 'bullet point' what they would like you to see. The Enthusiast wants you to relate to their excitement, to have some fun and interact. You may want you to join in their fun by looking for ways the group or team can interact occasionally. They truly do have some good ideas; they just need your direction to help keep them focused. The Enthusiast is a great starter, but not always a great finisher, and so set deadlines for them.

- Set deadlines for the Enthusiast.
- Ask for their ideas in writing so you have time to digest them.
- Join in and have some fun; you may even want to go for lunch or coffee and chat.

Ways for The Problem Solver to adapt and work better with The Enthusiast

- Enthusiasts can help keep your team get excited, especially around change, if you can get them on board.
- Remember: their intent is to interact, not to challenge you.

The Chief with The Friend

The Chief is typically a natural leader. You have a tendency to step up to the plate and take charge, especially when things aren't getting done. Your innate need is for results and when someone is holding up progress, your frustration may ignite. You have a tendency to be more demonstrative and can sometimes appear abrupt to the Friend. Your need to move forward on things to get something done is often completely different from how the Friend would handle it. The Friend may vacillate because they have an idea but are fearful that, because it doesn't match your idea, they will upset you; they are then reticent to bring it forward (delaying progress). When you find out, you are perplexed and you feel that they are being indecisive. When things don't go as planned, if the Friend is on your side, they have the ability to smooth things over for you; don't underestimate their loyalty, if you have it.

- Ensure the environment and your relationship is safe to bring ideas forward.
- Allow a longer time for Friends to express or articulate, as they will not always use the most direct approach.

Ways for The Chief to adapt and work better with The Friend

- In the event that you are not getting the idea, gently ask what they would like to see.
- Remember: their intent is to get along and have harmony and peace. They are the most steadfast, responsible and loyal individuals, if they support you.

The Friend with The Chief

The Friend is the most concerned about people and their feelings. In fact, you feel emotions at a very deep level yourself. You are a great humanitarian. You hate to let people down and will keep commitments. You are the most loyal, steadfast and reliable of the styles. When you can't keep people happy, you are often very hard on yourself. This tendency can sometimes make you retreat, especially around the Chief. You may find them abrupt, so you hold information back. The Chief can perceive this as being indecisive. Your methods or approach for accomplishing something are completely different. The Chief is often not angry with you personally, they are just frustrated when there are no immediate results. Their intent is to get it done. They will actually help you if you want them to. If you need something done, give it to the Chief. They won't let you down, they will get it done.

- Get to the point.
- Ask directly for what you need or want.
- Keep small talk to a minimum.
- State your ideas and demonstrate how they relate to results

Ways for The Friend to adapt and work better with The Chief

- Don't delay or put off things, you will gain more respect from the Chief.
- Remember: the intent of the Chief is to get results.

As you can see from all these styles, the intention behind each of our methods or approach is good. A thorough understanding of the good intentions behind each behavioral style will help you embrace and honor various styles, as opposed to getting angry at the different approaches. By the time we are five years old, most of our innate behaviors have been demonstrated. Parents with more than one child will see this, especially if their children are opposites.

WE NEED EVERY STYLE ON OUR TEAM

What would happen if we had all Chiefs on our team? We might all be vying for control—and you know what happens when there are too many cooks in the kitchen. What if we had all Friends on our team? We might not say anything or bring anything up, so as not to hurt anyone's feelings or upset things. You know, however, if we don't address conflicts and problems, bottlenecks occur. If we had all Problem Solvers on our team, would we get anything done? We would take our time and make sure everything was absolutely correct, which can cause missed deadlines. If we had all Enthusiasts on our team, would we get anything done? Well, we'd sure have fun trying to get the work done but that might not be enough.

Having a blend on the team will round things out. Everyone must have an appreciation for what each other brings to the table. That is why this understanding is so critical to a leader. Also if you are the leader in a position to build your team, be careful when selecting; you may just hire or bring a whole team of 'you' together and it might not serve you well.

I hope you've gleaned some useful information about the different types of people that make up your team. Once you learn to honor and embrace each and every style, even when it is not the method or approach you would take, try to understand the intent, and adapt or direct it. Whether a Chief, a Friend, an Enthusiast or a Problem Solver, you are the leader and good leaders utilize their team's assets and direct those talents accordingly. Women have been known to score higher on 'Emotional Intellegence' tests and I believe they have a unique talent in paying attention to assessing and evaluating themselves and others. The often deep need to nurture and care for others is inherent, and women can capitalize on this trait.

In the next chapter we will look at immediate challenges and the necessary transitions when you first step into the supervisory or managerial role. Even if you've been in the role for some time, managing friends or older, more experienced teams, and even professional jealousy can cause havoc. We'll discover some remarkable Velvet Hammer techniques for conquering these hurdles.

CHAPTER 3

Please Take out the Earrings

MANAGING FRIENDS, AND OTHER TRANSITIONS INTO MANAGEMENT

MANAGING FRIENDS

Are you just 'in charge' or are you ready to lead?

AS I mentioned, for two years I was a flight attendant with an amazing luxury charter airline back in the 80s. It was the days when airline travel was still pretty much a luxury. We served everything on Royal Doulton china and there was a hot meal or two on every flight. Everything about this airline was first class, including the expectations of the staff and their grooming regulations. A very dear friend of mine, a fellow 'senior' flight attendant, said, "You should go for the management job; you'd be really good at it!" So I did, and I got the job. It was scary at first, as I had to leave my secure union position and as a single mom, if I didn't make it, I felt I could be left in the cold. I was determined to make it. After a few weeks in training, it was time for my first flight.

It was a Boeing 747 going from Toronto to London, England. The things to think about were colossal; approximately 465 passengers, a dinner and breakfast flight, 15 very senior crew members, duty-free, customs and immigration paperwork with crew clearing and a myriad of other things I had to consider. Although anxious and somewhat flustered, I felt ready because of all the notes and preparations I had made. As I reviewed the crew schedule, I realized my friend was on the same flight; I was delighted and relieved that I'd have 'a friend' and an ally (at least, so I thought). We decided to save on parking and drive in together. On the way down the highway, I looked over at her while driving. To my amazement she was wearing 'non-regulation' oversized earrings. The chatter began in my head. "Should I say anything or not? She must know they aren't regulation. Oh—this is petty, leave it alone. You have too much to worry about today, focus on the flight preparation." I rehearsed the safety announcement in my head. It was a long drive to the airport.

Once in the briefing room, I looked around, ready to speak. There sat 15 very senior crew, all pressed and groomed. Those were the days when a crew walked through the airport like models on a runway. The crew looked sharp, but those earrings glared at me like they were six inches in diameter. As I began to review the services and safety procedures, I could feel the tension in the room. They knew, and were waiting for me to say something about the earrings. "Leave it alone," I told myself, "there are bigger things to deal with." I figured she knew and would take them out before the passengers arrived.

On board during pre-flight checks, I took the long walk down the aisle to the back galley where the crew were doing the count and checking safety equipment. When I arrived, the chatter stopped cold. I looked at them and smiled. No one spoke. They turned and continued with their tasks. I knew they knew. On the way back up the other aisle to where my friend was, I grabbed the courage to do my first 'fireside chat' as they had taught us in training. I looked at my friend and stated, "You're going to take those out, right"? She touched her earrings and said half-heartedly, "No, come on—it's you!" I grimaced and made another round down and back up the airplane. The passengers would be here any minute. The crew knew! I had to do something or there would have been a rush in London at *British Home Stores* jewelry department. On my second attempt, I got more 'assertive.' I said, "I need you to take those off!" She said, "No, I'm not going to." I said, "Then I'll have to document this!" She replied, "You don't have the guts."

The next two days were very long and several weeks later I realized my friend was no longer my friend. I was shocked and disappointed. She was the funniest, most outgoing person I'd ever met. We'd complain about ex-husbands, socialize and had even enjoyed traveling together. I felt this had been the nail in the coffin for the relationship. She was an amazing flight attendant and I thought a good friend. We have not spoken since.

YOU HAVE AN OBLIGATION TO YOUR ORGANIZATION FIRST

For years I'd wondered, did I do the right thing? Should I have not said anything? Was this petty, should I have let it go? As you mature in your leadership role, you will realize that if you've accepted the job as a supervisor, manager or leader, you have an obligation to the organization first to uphold standards. The organization typically builds itself on a certain reputation. This airline was 'classy' all the way; everything from meals to airplane cleanliness to the detailed grooming regulations often set it apart. Had there been a different focus, such as speed, efficiency, or affordability, as many of the airlines operate today, this situation may have never occurred. It just might not have been that important and I could have left it alone.

Know what your superiors, boss or organization expects, so you know when to step in and manage and what you can leave alone. It is often a fine line between firm and fair. Exercising good judgement and following your intuition (a fabulous female trait) will always help. I felt I did do the right thing after all. It was easy after that to correct grooming infractions; if I could address that situation, speaking to anyone else was easy.

Why is it so hard to manage friends? They expect different things from you. They know your weaknesses and can often expose them. If you manage friends or those with whom you socialize, you have to set up some ground rules. I now take my friends out for coffee early in my new role, and state, "From time to time, I will have to make difficult decisions, decisions you may not like. When those situations occur, can I ask for your understanding and support?"

Velvet Hammer Technique #5
SET GROUND RULES
AND GAIN SUPPORT UP FRONT.

I often feel that if I had had this conversation over coffee or even breakfast that morning with my friend, I could have garnered her support upfront and prevented the situation altogether. Once you've done this, as difficult situations arise you can gently remind them, "This is one of those situations we talked about. Can you help me out?" If left until after the situations hit you, you are managing by pushing, instead of pulling.

MANAGING OLDER, EXPERIENCED PEOPLE

The same holds true for managing older, experienced people. Guess what—they often *do* know more than you! Why wouldn't they? They've been there longer, they know the skeletons, what worked and what didn't and often why. Sometimes, they even applied for your job and didn't get it, and then you are also dealing with rivalry or jealousy. What do you do now?

Tap into their experience. They are the 'subject matter experts.' Set ground rules with them too. I often ask them to go for lunch or coffee. Informal settings seem to work best. I ask for their input and ideas and admit that I'm new, and that I couldn't possibly know everything out of the gate. I call upon them for their expertise in certain areas, and ask if they would help or bring things to my attention.

One thing you have to be careful of is: if you lean too much on them, your staff or subordinates may start going to them instead of you for direction. If you see this happening, ensure you step back in and start asking more questions and getting input from all the staff to aid in your learning curve. You may have to ask the experienced person to send the people your way and/or keep you informed of any directions given. You will slowly start taking the helm again as your learning curve increases. Again, set up the ground rule as to when you need your older, experienced staff to give direction or not and when to send people your way.

Velvet Hammer Technique #6
**TAP INTO EXISTING EXPERTISE
AND KNOWLEDGE.**

MANAGING THE YOUNG AND INEXPERIENCED

A final challenge is the new hiree who is inexperienced, or is very young and may not have the professional maturity to know it is not okay to fold their arms or roll their eyes like they do at their mother. You may even have some forty-year-old 'four-year-olds' that are still rolling their eyes in meetings (read Chapter 7 on discipline to see how to deal with these behaviors). With inexperienced people, get them learning as quickly as possible. Always make extra time, even if it is asking them to spend 15 minutes before or after work for a few days, or have lunch with them to conduct an orientation. Always describe the reason the job exists and the primary goals that are to be accomplished. Go through any regulations, standards or policies, even if they've been through formal training, and do a quick review of their knowledge by asking them questions. Participants typically only retain about 10% to 40% (if you are lucky) of what they learned, depending on how the training is delivered. Have them take notes or offer short, quick abbreviated job aids for any technical type of training or things that must be remembered, but don't overload the information.

Often you will have to repeat yourself, re-word things, or offer diagrams. People learn at different rates and in different ways (visual, auditory, hands on). Give them early responsibility and ownership for doing the job. I often won't accept "I'm new" or "I don't know how." That is my cue to prepare job aids, checklists or prompters or get them some form of more formal training. Training may seem labor intensive, but if you don't do it, you will spend more time re-hiring or doing re-work. I frequently pair people with someone senior for job shadowing or job mirroring, if and when I can. We actually learn better from mistakes, so allow or build time in for this when you can. Of course, don't go too fast, as injury could occur, or a life could be endangered.

Velvet Hammer Technique #7
TEACH AND TRAIN UP FRONT.

WHAT TO SAY ON THE FIRST DAY

One of the greatest 'fear factor' days I remember having is deciding what to say to my new team on the first day, especially when I was very 'green.' When I was volunteering as president of a non-profit group, I remember being fearful of how I'd come across, especially to those I considered to be my peer group and very knowledgeable. In volunteer organizations you don't really have 'true' authority to hire and fire volunteers, and if you do push too hard, they quit. My goal as a leader has always been to have people to follow (pull, not push). I believe you are only a true leader when your team is ready to follow. So how do you get them ready? By listening! Listening, which is covered in greater detail in Chapter 6, is the greatest skill I learned as a leader (and those who know me wish I could still get better at it). With my great need to connect with people and interact, I always thought I should do the talking; especially if there was dead air. I'd fill it—often quickly. This does not work. People will shut down. Watch how it happens in a meeting, do all the talking and then ask if there are any questions... there is no need for anyone to add anything, you've just done it all. Even though I often know the answers, I still ask first.

Velvet Hammer Technique #8
ASK! DON'T TELL!

Here are some concrete tips you can use on your first day:

(1) Visit with your boss, superior or board, and clarify:
- What are the most important aspects of this role?
- If I could improve one thing in this area, department, or organization, what would that be?
- Where do you think I will excel and where do you think I will need help?

(2) Hold a meeting with your team and discuss:
- What do they like/dislike about how things are being done?
- What would they like to change and not change?
- Discuss your goals, expectations and how you would like them to communicate ideas.

A good rule of thumb is to write their comments down for your future reference. If there is disagreement in the group, you will pick up on this right away. Set a ground rule; the meeting is to get ideas and feedback.

Don't make any decisions at this time (you may need permission or more information about situations). Let the team know you are new and don't have all the answers. Let them know that you may come to them from time to time for their input, explanations and expertise.

Be upfront when you do make mistakes, especially during your learning curve, and when mistakes occur, do everything to correct them, or prevent them from happening in the future. If you have time, try to spend informal time with each team member in a private setting to discuss their ideas more openly.

Remember, the best way to treat all these situations during your transition to being a leader is to set ground rules first. Ask for what you need, ask for input, ideas or someone's thoughts on a situation. Velvet Hammers look for ways to develop people by asking, getting to know them; they can teach you a lot if you listen. Read on to find out how Velvet Hammers plan, schedule and get the work done—on time.

CHAPTER 4

Playing With No Nets

SETTING THE STAGE

NETS ALLOW PEOPLE TO SCORE AND WIN!

Know where you want to go—before you get there!

IF a team was playing basketball with no nets (goals), what would that look like? Would it look like the area you are trying to organize and lead? Without nets (like basketball nets), teams don't know where to shoot. They just go off on tangents and make things up. They run up and down the court with no direction. Unsure what is important or not, they turn left when you thought they should go right and then everyone gets burned out, frustrated and sometimes they quit (even without handing in their notice.) They show up for the paycheck or other

49

perceived reward, but they don't put in their best effort—they quit internally and then you have to spend extra time 'motivating' and putting out fires.

One of the first things you'll want to be crystal clear about when leading others, so you can manage effectively, is why the organization exists. What is your organization's relevance? Do you know what you and your team are aiming for? What do you truly provide and for whom? Once you can answer these fundamental questions, managing and leading becomes easy. You'll know what to focus on and where to discipline, guide and direct.

In my seminars I often ask the group, "Who would like to play basketball?" They invariably put up their hands, as they see I have a small toy basketball in my hand and they think it is going to be fun. I break them into two teams. I state the rules: "Today we are going to play basketball, the only thing is, there are no nets." I throw the ball into the group and the person who catches it is encouraged to throw the ball and get the game going. I clap my hands wildly as they throw the ball and give lots of encouragement and support. It is fun for about 30 seconds.

By the time the third person throws the ball, they look at me like I'm crazy. Now, I'm a good coach, so I plead and cheer them on to keep going. They reluctantly throw the ball (and may even roll their eyes). Finally, the rebel in the crowd (do you have one on your team?) slams the ball down on their table and says, "This is dumb, I'm not doing it, you are wasting my time." I again encourage and coach them, I may even take them aside and coach them some more. They throw the ball again with as little effort as possible to the next person (usually right beside them, as if to say, "Get this off my desk as fast as possible, this is boring"). Do you have staff like this?

Once again, I'm successful in getting the teams to play, but it is a lot of effort and, frankly, I'm exhausted and it is getting to be not much fun for me either. Finally someone in the crowd (*and this happens every time*), always my most 'creative genius' (do you have one on your team?), takes the initiative and without even asking first, gets the ball and says, "I know, let's pretend there are nets," and points to where the imaginary nets are on the walls. The crowd follows his or her lead. S/he throws the ball and all of a sudden the group comes alive again. They start scoring and keeping score. They are giving each other high fives, cheering, smiling and really putting in an incredible effort.

I watch this in amazement every time and I'm not exhausted anymore, I'm elated that my team is motivated. Then all of a sudden I pretend to realize something. I say to the audience in horror, "Oh no, wait a minute, the rules are '**there are no nets**'. Who told you there were nets? Now we have to start all over again." Do you have people on your team who make up their own nets? Do they go left instead of right, and you are thinking, "What planet are you on? Who told you to do that?"

People instinctively want to contribute; they want to succeed. Alternatively, if there are no nets, people will give up and put no effort into their work. It is boring, tedious and feels like a waste of time. Think of a time when you felt your tasks had no meaning—no nets?

Velvet Hammer Technique #9
SET UP NETS – GOALS FOR YOUR TEAM!

SETTING THE STAGE, SO YOU
CAN SET NETS (GOALS)

Let me ask you this—why does your organization, business or association exist? Name them in 2 or 3 adjectives (see examples below if you need more idea of what I mean).

_____

_____

_____

Let me give you some examples of this. McDonald's restaurants exist to be:
- Affordable
- Fast, efficient
- Clean *(at least they always used to be, if you remember the old commercials where the guys were always cleaning the grills, mopping the floors and then sliding across the floors in those pointed hats).*

When McDonald's was created, I'm sure the creator of the business was sick of burger joints that were inefficient, overpriced and frankly had greasy windows. I've heard that the creator wanted to fix this for *their* customers, so he created McDonald's.

Let's look at another example for illustrative purposes (and this is my opinion only). Holland America Cruise Lines in the 1980s vs. Carnival Cruise Lines. Things may have changed as their markets changed.

Holland America Cruise Lines (in my opinion) was known for:
- Luxury
- Elegance

Carnival Cruise Lines (in my opinion) was known for:
- Fun
- Affordability

They had two different target markets and existed to service these markets. If you were a manager on Holland America Cruise Lines, could the employees have worn baseball hats? Would you have to manage this if they did? On Carnival could they have? I'm not 100% sure, but when I went on cruises in the 80s, the staff on some of the excursions from Carnival Cruise Lines were having so much fun with their patrons, they not only wore a baseball cap, they even turned the baseball cap backwards (especially when doing the limbo on the Tiki-Tiki flat-bottomed boat excursion). Again, this is only my observation; the people were having fun with their guides and grooming regulations (elegance) did not seem to be as important as fun, which was their market. Can you imagine someone from Holland America doing this, let alone an employee wearing a baseball cap backwards? It is easy to manage and set expectations when you know why you exist.

Why does your organization, association or group exist? What is your relevance? What do the people, members or customers receive from you? Have you listed three adjectives that set nets?

More examples (my opinion as a consumer):
- **Southwest Airlines:** Affordable, fun, on time
- **American Airlines:** Global, connections, on time

A conversation to correct employees who waste time, fool around or dawdle in an airline might sound like this:

"We are known (or *want to be known*), for **on-time performance** and **affordable pricing,** we need a concerted effort towards efficiency as we strive for the best on-time performance. When a customer misses their connection, we have to compensate and then struggle to keep our prices affordable." (Then track on-time performance and share numbers with employees).

A Church Organization: Community, support, faith
A conversation to manage volunteers who don't follow through with commitments may sound like this:

"We are known for our **support in the community;** when a volunteer doesn't follow through, we let the community or a church member down, and risk losing the very membership we exist to support." (Then track volunteers' efforts and contributions to the meetings, contributions, etc.).

WHY YOUR DEPARTMENT EXISTS

Once you have recognized this for your company, drill down into why your department exists.

Examples:

- **Accounting**: Accurate, efficient, profits
- **Marketing**: Growth, profits, recognizable (brand)
- **Operations**: Safety, production, efficiency

List 2 or 3 adjectives describing why your department exists:

_____

_____

_____

SETTING NETS (GOALS)

Once you know why the organization and the department or area exist, set goals with your team. I look for things that are broken or areas in which we are not justifying the reason we exist. I ask, "What is stopping us from accomplishing a great safety record, accuracy, increased sales or membership, etc.?" Many times you will find out what is broken by asking your team. Find out what they are frustrated with, such as equipment breaking down, systems not working, reports being late, deadlines being missed, absence of documentation, lack of training, being short staffed. Often we want to blame a team member for things breaking down or not getting done. If you look at the net, or lack of the net, it will help you focus on the outcome, not the person.

Velvet Hammer Technique #10
FOCUS ON OUTCOMES, NOT THE PERSON!

SETTING GOOD OLD-FASHIONED GOALS

Once I understand the areas for improvement, where I need to set up nets, I set up goals using the method outlined below, which clearly outlines the steps in goal setting. It is as follows:

Definable: The goal has to be clear to everyone by making it well defined.

An example of a poorly set goal: "We'd like to improve communication." This won't work as it is too vague. Often when there is a communication breakdown you feel like it is company-wide (and often organizations spend thousands of dollars trying to correct this). I'm called in all the time to do communications training. Communication breakdowns typically come from a *system breakdown* or when someone doesn't *truly know what the expectation is*. We discuss this further in Chapter 6 on how things are misconstrued when we explore how people communicate.

To show you how this works for goal setting, in my seminars I often ask a participant to explain an example of a communication breakdown. They invariably tell me how someone is missing a deadline, walking by broken equipment, not paying attention to accuracy, and a whole range of other issues. Once we can 'peel away the onion' and get to the heart of the communication issue, then we can start to make a goal definable. To make the communication problem better defined, let's use accuracy on reports as the cause of the communication problem.

Example of Definable: "Improve the accuracy of report xyz."

The next step is:

Quantifiable. You have to find a way to measure your goal so you know if things are getting better. For example, you will have to find out how bad things are regarding the accuracy of the reports. In other words, to find out by how much you'd like to improve the accuracy, you will need to record the error rate for a period of time. Then you can get a benchmark and set a *quantifiable* goal.

Example of Quantifiable: "Improve the accuracy rate on report *xyz* by 25%." Maybe it is the number of customer complaints you'd like to improve.

Definable and quantifiable: "Decrease the number of customer complaints by xyz%." Whatever you do, try to come up with a number around the issue you are trying to correct. If it is a restaurant, maybe it is bathrooms that are to be cleaned consistently every hour, 98% of the time. You'd then set up some form of tracking system to make sure you goal is monitored.

Velvet Hammer Technique #11
WHAT GETS MEASURED GETS ATTENTION!

The next step is:

Attainable: You will want to make sure it is attainable. Don't set the goal too high or too low. For instance, if you want 100% accuracy, the first time someone makes a mistake (and they will), the goal is over. The team is demotivated. If it is too low, the day they hit the number, they give up trying, you stop measuring and it goes by the wayside. Be very practical when setting this number. I usually try to reach a consensus with the team on the number.

Example of Attainable: "Improve the error rate by 25%."

The next step is:

Practical. Make sure the goal is within your area of responsibility and that it is indeed practical. If it is another department's issue, that is a different skill you'll need, which I discuss in Chapter 6 on communication. If it is not within your realm of control, you can't set the goal and of course your team cannot hit the net, and typically everyone will just get frustrated. Avoid this by ensuring the goal is practical and within your control. If breakdowns are occurring inter-departmentally, perhaps you could develop a joint goal.

The final step is:

Deadline: I've always heard that a goal is not a goal without a deadline. You must know the time at which you need to reach your goal (again, make sure it is attainable and practical when you set a date). Have you ever found you've been unsuccessful in losing weight or quitting smoking? Often it is because you don't know by 'when' you would like to accomplish this. Yet, if there was a wedding, a vacation or a birthday, you'd have a date and you would be more likely to accomplish your goal. A deadline or a date as to when you would like everyone to accomplish the goal gives everyone a clear target. Could you imagine playing basketball with no timekeeper, in a game with no timeframe or ending? How motivated do you think the team would be to accomplish anything? This is why you can sometimes hear your staff saying, "Who cares? Different day, same ____." If there are no nets, no goals, everyone feels lost and no one cares about fixing anything, so why should they? Watch your team step up to the plate when you set a couple of goals per quarter, or each year, for your team.

Example of Deadline: "By June 30th, we will have improved the error rate on xyz reports by 25%." Then track, reward and celebrate as you move forward.

Don't set more than three goals at a time; it becomes overwhelming for the team. Once you've hit them, choose new goals, so the team has something to aim for. There is always room for improvement in any organization. In the next chapter we'll discuss how motivating this is, and then how to reward and recognize your teams and individuals as they hit the nets.

Some sample goals:
- Increase the memberships by 25% by year end.
- Decrease the error rate on xyz reports by June 30th, XXXX.
- Decrease equipment breakdowns by 20% by the end of next quarter.
- Improve attendance by 12% by year end.

- Decrease the accident rate in the warehouse by 10% by March 15 xxxx.

Once you have set the goal, you can use the work-sheets provided in the next section to get your staff involved in the next steps and what might have to take place to accomplish the goal. By getting your team involved in the process, they are better equipped to help out and be able to **contribute**.

GETTING THE WORK DONE THROUGH DELEGATION

Putting a plan together and delegating so we can get our work done, meet goals and continue to manage and be available for our team is an absolute requirement when leading others. If you don't delegate, you will get burned out and often become resentful. Women, being the great multi-taskers they are, can get sidetracked or pulled into doing it all themselves. You often hear that it is faster to do it yourself, that they might not do it as well as you can, or that it is just easier to do it yourself.

Let's use a common project example to illustrate how we can delegate eloquently and ensure it gets done: a new computer system will be installed in the next two months. In a meeting, I make the announcement (everyone will groan). Your goal might be: the new computer system will be successfully installed on 95% of all computers by June 30th. Together we agree on the goal, with specifics and a deadline. I use a whiteboard, flipchart or overhead transparency with the following template:

SAMPLE GOAL SETTING AND DELEGATION TEMPLATE

GOAL: By the end of the third quarter, the XYZ computer system will be installed on 36 machines. All users will be competently trained to service customers, track transactions and print reports, with an error rate no higher than 20%.

A	B	C	D
Tasks	Who	Deadline	√ Check when completed.
1. Audit of current computers and systems	Mary	April 15	Note: The manager uses this column to ensure dead-lines are met. *(This should be the only column that the manager's name goes on).*
2. Training schedule defined, communicated and tracked.	Sylvia	April 20	
3. Training or job aids developed (if not provided by vendor). (Note: I'm only listing 3 samples to illustrate this point)	Susan	May 15	

SOME TIPS WHEN YOU USE THIS GOAL-SETTING DELEGATION APPROACH.

a) Identify the tasks that have to be completed first (you will probably keep adding as you go along). Use **column A**

b) Ask for volunteers for each task (remember there will be sub-tasks that can go under each heading, either at the time or later on). Try to spread the wealth; you may have to put two or more individuals together on a task. If someone volunteers their name for the task, as opposed to you assigning it to them, they are more apt to complete it. **Use column B**

c) If there are people on your team that have not volunteered for a task and you think they should be fulfilling an obligation (think teamwork), then you may want to ask which area they would like to assist with or delegate by adding their name to a task. If they disagree with the one you've put their name down for, ask them which task they feel best suited to do. (If they flat-out refuse, you may want to read Chapter 8.)

d) Try not to put your name down under any of the tasks, just use column D for managing the task. The one thing you should concentrate on is putting the check beside the task as it is done. Your job is to ensure the tasks get completed by the deadline.

e) Make sure you put a deadline beside each task; you will see where things have to be adjusted. This will be your area to manage—the deadlines. (Tip: Set 'false' deadlines if you have to, a couple of days or hours earlier, to give yourself some breathing room, but don't publicly announce this or everyone will get used to not taking the deadline seriously). **Use column C**

f) Once everyone has agreed with the template, you will have to ensure that each person knows how to get started and be available for helping them get the resources, templates and information they need to succeed. Check in often, but be aware of when you are nagging.

g) Check when each task is scheduled to be done and if necessary move the date to accommodate schedules or change who is doing what task. **Use column D**

h) Put the project plan on your wall and note follow-ups in a day planner or calendar. Don't show up on the day of the deadline and ask, "Have you done that?" Ensure you check in early enough to intervene so you can offer the guidance or assistance they need to succeed in the task.

j) Hold a quick meeting for updates on everyone's progress.

This is the pull vs. push method to delegation, and a great way to project plan at the same time. Not only will you need to allocate resources, tasks and deadlines, you may also want input on costs, barriers and any other dependencies amongst team members and/or other departments.

Velvet Hammer Technique #12
DELEGATE SO YOU CAN MANAGE!

BUDGET TIPS

Often a manager is responsible for setting and submitting a budget for work assignments. I remember one manager who told me that when they were asked to do this the first time they had no idea how to do it, and grabbed a set of dice and rolled, and then filled in the numbers. This was for a major international company (I won't say which, as most people would recognize it). Just a warning—it does go on. To complete a budget, if there are direct costs that you will be submitting and controlling, take a look at all the tasks and build the costs around that. If you've never had to prepare a budget for your area it can seem daunting. Let me show you how easy it can be if you are ever asked. Think of how you would budget for an event; it is very similar for your organization or your area of responsibility.

Hotel conference room(s):	$_____
Meals:	$_____
Marketing or announcements:	$_____
Gifts or door prizes:	$_____
Misc. (taxes, gratuities, etc.)	$_____
Contingency	$_____

Just list as many expenses as you think you may have or will need. If you have an accounting department or an accounting chairperson on your board, have them assist you. If organizations don't watch their spending they will quickly find themselves without the funding to continue. Without prior planning and a good idea of spending controls, managers or leaders with the authority to spend their organization's funds must be prudent or they may help the very organization they are trying to help go under.

If things grow or spiral out of your control when you are leading, you will be able to make decisions quickly on whether you can afford things, continue with the project, modify it or request further funding. There are many ways to do your own budget. Just sit down and list your items and costs. Get several quotes. I like to get three quotes and compare deliverables (what I'm getting) and the different price points. Often your accounting department will provide you with worksheets, so work with them closely, if you can get access to them. If you don't have one, don't get sidetracked by not having a budget or an idea of your spending. You may also want to add a margin for contingency or 'extras' that might arise beyond your control.

Velvet Hammer Technique #13
**CONTROL SPENDING ON THE RIGHT THINGS
— MAKE A PLAN!**

CONTRIBUTION—A STRONG MOTIVATOR FOR WOMEN

I've not proven this, it is only a hunch based on numerous observations, but it appears that one of the greatest motivators for women is the need to contribute. I often wonder if women have a strong need to provide service and a strong yearning to make a difference, not only in our work but in our families, and that is perhaps why we seem to have the challenge with 'work–life balance,' more so than men. If you don't believe me, just look at how many seminars and conferences on work–life balance are attended by men; I'm not saying they don't struggle, it just seems to be required predominantly by women. I know that I'm always stretching my time to keep things in place, make people happy and feel satisfied to finish things and know I helped in some way. I would like to say that delegation is a great way to help feed this need and allows women to make a contribution. I suggest that whenever you can, get women to contribute and when they can see the results of their contributions you will have a very motivated team. It may be evolutionary, as we've always seemed to have enjoyed cooking and preparing things communally throughout the ages. It did—and I believe it still does—take a village.

In the next chapter we are going to explore how Velvet Hammers keep their teams motivated and contributing, even when budgets are tight. In Chapter 9 I briefly discuss work–life balance (as I know you probably don't have a lot of time).

CHAPTER 5

When Lap Dancing Won't Do

MOTIVATION AND CONTRIBUTION

WHERE MOTIVATION COMES FROM

Motivation comes from within the individual—but a good leader knows they have influence.

AS we learned in Chapter 4, setting and monitoring concrete goals often allows a leader to recognize and reward the most important areas that have the greatest impact, and determine where the greatest contributions are being made. I believe that the number one motivational factor in today's workforce is *contribution*, not money, and as I mentioned, I feel this is a strong need in women. Now we've learned how to capitalize on this by setting goals and allowing people to contribute through a work plan. By focusing on the real results of these targets and goals it becomes easy and affordable to recognize people for their contributions, which often cost the organization pennies, not raises. Mind you, if you take the money away or don't stay market competitive with the industry you are in, they may leave. I'm not saying money isn't important, I'm just saying it's not the most important thing. We'll talk about non-profits and volunteers later.

Velvet Hammer Technique #14
BEING ABLE TO CONTRIBUTE, NOT MONEY, IS ONE OF THE GREATEST MOTIVATORS.

Think about it, though—when was the last time you got a raise? How long did the euphoria last? One week, two months or a bit longer, before you said to yourself during a crisis or difficult challenge, "This job doesn't pay me enough"? If you are a non-profit and leading as a volunteer and managing volunteers, if they are not motivated, they quit, don't show up, let you down and then you are often doing the work yourself. Contribution, being able to make a difference, I believe is the number one motivational factor today, because most of us already have our shelter and basic needs looked after.

REWARDING & RECOGNIZING CONTRIBUTION

Think of a young kid who is working in a minimum wage job and doesn't feel they contribute. They get bored and often lethargic towards their responsibilities. Once you stop contributing, you stop learning, and once your brain stops learning, it shrinks and often becomes cranky. How much fun will you be to have around? It is the same with your staff. They need to be challenged, continue learning and to have goals. This keeps people motivated. Have you ever done something so often that if you had to do it one more day you'd cry?

By understanding why your organization and team exists, as discussed in the previous chapter, you realize that you must have goals or targets. When you meet these goals or even make progress towards hitting these goals, you can have a party, a celebration, something to recognize and thank individual or team efforts, then your team and individuals usually become or stay motivated. When they are recognized they take pride in their work and become very motivated.

Just think about it—when was the last time you were recognized? You felt great! What happens when no one notices your efforts? You give up and think, "Who cares? No one notices anyway." A warning here: if you have stepped into the leadership role you may not be recognized as frequently as you would like. As you are the leader, often there is no one in your vicinity directly watching your accomplishments. Don't be disturbed by this, just look at the goals you and the team are hitting and be proud as this happens. When your team or department accomplishes something, ensure when you tell your superior that you use the word 'we' or 'them,' not 'I.'

CONTINUOUS LEARNING IS A GREAT MOTIVATOR

Another great motivator, aside from meeting goals and being able to make a contribution, is continuous learning. Have you allowed your team to develop in different areas? Have they done the same job for so long they could cry? Are they bored out of their wits? Often when this happens they look for things that are wrong and can become quite cranky, too. In other words, they've retired without handing in their notice. Try getting them to learn a new task or switch tasks with someone else, so they can help during vacations or absences. Expand their job somehow so they take on new roles.

When change occurs in an organization, embrace it, as it gives everyone the opportunity to learn new things. It might not be easy at first, but if change is handled well and new learning is supported, individuals and teams can blossom. If you have the budget, send your staff to training programs, even senior long-term employees. Learning something new keeps people motivated.

The other reason you want to keep developing people is so you have someone prepared for succession planning. I've been involved in the decision-making process where we could not promote a manager as there was no one qualified to take their position. They often wonder why they didn't get the job, even though they were qualified. Make sure you have employees developed to do your job, so you can move on (and also go on vacation without facing all that work when you get back).

Velvet Hammer Technique #15
LEARNING SHOULD BE LIFELONG!

DELEGATION AS A MOTIVATOR

Delegating tasks to other people is another great motivator and, as discussed above, it not only helps you go on vacation with ease, but it helps you develop people so you can move on in your career. How does one delegate successfully so this can happen? First of all, give up your fears of delegation, which typically include the following:

- They might make a mistake or do it all wrong.
- What if it is such a mess it will take me twice as long to correct it? (I hate rework too!)
- It will take longer for me to train them than to just do it myself.

The benefits of delegating and getting staff developed in all areas by far outweigh the above fears. Are the fears real? Yes, and it may happen, so take the time to schedule the development and go for it.

First, make a list of everything you do and who might be the best person to develop, and note when might be a good time to get them trained or started on this learning.

Guidelines:
- Ensure you have someone who would be able to do each task or has the ability to learn it.
- Determine when would be a good time to conduct the training or discussions on how to do the task.
- Perhaps don't delegate the entire job, but just small components of it.

> The only things you cannot delegate are things that are of a personal or confidential nature, or anything that is regulated by a required license or certification.

Tasks You Do	Delegate to Whom	Delegate When

Now that you have an idea of what can be delegated and to whom, start scheduling for this to happen. As different demands on your time crop up, you will be glad you did it, as you can delegate certain tasks during high-churn times. What happens if someone says, "That is not my job!"? Remember the first Velvet Hammer technique: set expectations. Make sure you get agreement from the team member that they are interested in learning a new task before you delegate it to them. Demanding that someone does something often won't work, especially for a woman. Culturally, it is not accepted. I often point out how learning new things will assist them in their own personal development and help everyone during absences and vacations. I ensure the learning curve is supported and reiterate that it is okay to make mistakes. Of course, if someone's life or physical safety is at risk, extra care and supervision are required.

A quick checklist I use when I'm training someone in a new task:

a) Ask them what they know about the task already (check for understanding so you know where to start and don't over-detail the task when you train).

b) Describe why the task exists and what it is designed to accomplish (what and why).

c) Describe any deadlines or timeframes for the task to be completed (when).

d) Describe who else is depending on the task (who).

e) Describe where the task should be conducted (where).

f) I then demonstrate the task and stop to ask questions for understanding along the way (usually where, what, why, when questions).

g) I then ask them to demonstrate it back (so I can offer feedback or correction along the way).

Be sure to be available for questions. If you find you are constantly being interrupted, ask them to set aside a series of questions and to come to you with them all at once at a mutually agreed time. Delegation can seem tricky at first, but it is often motivating to the employee and a luxury for you.

COST-EFFECTIVE RECOGNITION & REWARD

Some of the questions I often get are, "What is the best way to reward and recognize my staff? What works and what backfires? How do I make it cost effective, especially if I am part of a non-profit organization and sometimes the reward may have to come out of my own pocket or the membership's?" Many corporations have tried hugely expensive corporate incentives programs, only to have them backfire. Some organizations (for example, I understand some governments with union employees are not allowed to reward or recognize staff in any way as it may show discrimination or favoritism). I think this is a great shame and I hope governments and unions will examine this policy and other options in the future.

In my seminars I often ask managers how they recognize and reward staff, so I can capture great ideas and pass them on to other managers—there are so many creative, affordable and inexpensive ways to reward and recognize teams and individuals. Just be careful what you choose to use as your reward—you don't want to get in trouble, even though you think it is cute. See the list of ideas from participants that follows in this chapter.

WHY LAP DANCING CAN BE A PROBLEM

In one public seminar I had a group of men giggling in the back of the room when I asked this question, "How do you motivate your staff, and in what creative way do you recognize and reward employees?" When I asked them to share they said, "We provide **lap dancing** to the employee of the month." Now if you don't know what lap dancing is, it typically involves men going to an establishment (usually where alcohol is served), and a scantily dressed woman dancing for the men, and sitting on the lap of a man while dancing provocatively. (I've never been, but they've told me this is what happens). I'm assuming for this group of men it may have been quite motivating. The Human Resource Managers in the room nearly fall out of their chairs.

The reason Human Resources Managers do this is that they know how it might play out. The man comes home from work all happy that he won 'Employee of the Month'. The wife says, "Wow, honey, that is great, what did you win?" The husband flushes red and says, "Now honey, don't get upset, it is very much a guy thing." She says, "So, what did you get?" He mumbles, "Lap dancing. I hated it, but I had to go, it was with the guys and all, you know how it is, don't get upset." She says, "Did you really hate it?" He proclaims, "Yes honey, it was awful, but my boss was there, the guys—you can imagine, I just had to go along with it." She states again, "Are you sure you really hated it?" He says, "Yes, honey, it was awful, I really hated it." She says, "Fine, then that is coercion, we're suing their butts off."

Be very careful what you use to reward your staff. You may say, "I think my team needs a round of Cosmopolitans (a fancy martini-type drink)." It may be a very social and fun reward, but be careful—if someone gets into an accident, your company may be held responsible. Anything that you think might be cute, if it is questionable, I'd warn you to stay away from it. Also ask, is it politically correct?

When recognizing individuals and teams, ensure you state the contribution and the impact it had. Be careful not to miss this step or it can come out like false praise. "Atta boy" and "Way to go" without stating what and how can leave employees confused.

Velvet Hammer Technique #16
WHEN RECOGNIZING PEOPLE, ENSURE YOU STATE THE CONTRIBUTION AND THE IMPACT IT HAD.

Here is a list of fun, affordable ways to reward and recognize teams and individuals that have come up in my seminars. Select things that you think will work for your team—you may even ask them what they may like. Find out what might be suitable or how your employee would like to be recognized, or it may backfire on you. Here are some ideas:

- An email thanking them for their contribution and efforts (state what and how they contributed). This is not only free, but it also may work in government and union workplaces.

- A small thank you card (same as above)

- Small chocolate, a flower (something women don't get enough of, I'm told in my research)

- Movie certificates

- Coffee cards

- 'Way to go' stickers (or themed stickers if you've themed your goal or incentive program)

- Beanie Baby or small stuffed toy in the character of what you want to recognize (example: a lion symbolizing the lion's share of the work).

- Coffee mugs

- Interesting or unique jewelry (go to www.thevelvethammer.com) to find unique Velvet Hammer jewelry for the woman who just got a promotion!)

- A training program (book, CD, DVD)

- Local sports or theatre tickets (especially if they've worked a lot of overtime for you—when you give them the gift, write an accompanying note stating, "Since I took you away from your family, please have some time back with them.")

- Car wash certificates

- Corporate gifts from the marketing department (bags, hats, shirts, etc.). (Make sure there is a budget for this and don't inundate the marketing department with requests.)

- Bake cookies for your team and bring them in—or better yet, if you have a staff room with an oven, put them in just before coffee break and have the aroma waft through the office. If they get used to this being a reward for something the team has done right, they'll start feeling great for fifteen minutes before they know the recognition is coming.

- Food or some type of social celebration always works (barbeques, pot lucks, fresh fruit tray, even donuts).

- Add your own list of ideas here:

Remember to recognize and reward contributions of individuals and teams. Have you ever wondered when you should recognize someone publicly vs. privately? A few tips here:

When to recognize publicly:

- The person enjoys and sometimes needs the attention.

- Teams when they reach goals or start on their way to the goal.

- When individuals demonstrate contributions that are above and beyond the norm.

When to recognize privately:

- When you've corrected someone's performance privately and they are now showing great gains toward fixing the issue (for example, if you publicly praise this individual for now meeting the standard, and everyone else demonstrates this behavior on an ongoing basis anyway, the rest of your team will be demotivated as they could feel, "Well, I do that all the time and no one ever notices me."). Make sure you do recognize the employee who has made the corrections in their performance, just do it privately.

- When an individual would be mortified by the attention (be careful, as even the most shy people will put up a fuss about getting the attention, but most secretly enjoy public praise). Be aware of cultural issues. If you are unsure, ask the person privately if they mind being recognized publicly. It does ruin the element of surprise, but it is more respectful.

• When you have someone that constantly gets attention, but the rest of the team are frustrated by the constant 'wins' of this person (usually a strong player).

Velvet Hammers find out what their teams want and know what makes them tick. They find out what 'motivates' and what doesn't. Then they watch to catch people doing things right and celebrate it. In the next chapter we explore how things get miscommunicated, how conflict eats away at a team and individuals, and how it creates negativity and demotivates. A Velvet Hammer has the skills to conquer this and pulls even the most difficult teams together.

CHAPTER 6

It Doesn't Matter if You Are Right

HANDLING CONFLICT AND TEAM CONFLICT WITH GRACE

FINDING THIRD WAYS

The ability to handle conflict gracefully is the greatest skill of all.

ONE of the greatest skill sets I believe a woman leader can master is the technique of handling conflict eloquently. Do you find it is hard not to bring your work conflicts home or alternatively, not to bring your conflicts from home to your work? They often overlap. The skills discussed in this chapter will help you in both places. I believe it is our hormones at work here. You rarely see men discussing their issues with a group of people. When we don't understand the simple causes of conflict and simple methods to deal with it eloquently, we can find ourselves caught up in ongoing quarrels that can eat away at our productivity and can exacerbate our mental state. We are more emotional than men. Unfortunately, throughout our education most of us never learned how to deal with conflict, so we handle it like we learned at home and we get what we get from others, who also lack skills in handling conflict.

When conflict arises, you will see groups of women getting involved. They will often bring it to the attention of others and seek support; remember our hormones discussed in Chapter 1, the need to 'talk about it and befriend' especially when upset or stressed (remember our oxytocin levels?). Often the angst at 'the water cooler' can be targeted at the boss, supervisor, manager or leader. Things can get really messy, especially if the leader attempts to step in to help during third-party conflicts, takes sides or appears to take sides. I truly hope women can understand that this behavior does not help us adapt (I too still get caught up in it from time to time, as I just need to vent). Ever feel like you are in a scene from the movie 'Mean Girls'? If you manage a team, set up some ground rules for discussing and resolving conflicts.

DOES IT MATTER IF YOU ARE RIGHT?

To illustrate several points about conflict, let me tell you a love story between a man and his wife, and a man and his mother. Every summer I went to my husband's cabin up north for our family vacation. This is where he spent every summer, from June to September, every year of his childhood. It was a five-hour drive, and then we would unload for a forty-minute boat ride, as the cabin sat on an island about the size of a football field in the middle of a river. The bass fishing was perhaps the best in the world, or so they (my husband and his brothers) claimed. The cabin (a hut) was over 100 years old and had been in his family for three generations. It had no running water, no electricity, an outhouse and mosquitoes as large as your children. My husband loved it; I hated it. But I went because it was my family vacation and I wanted to support the second thing he loved most in the world; his family, of course, came first.

One year on the way up, about an hour into the drive, my husband looked at me and said, "I forgot to tell you, my mom is coming." Now, I love, respect and truly admire my mother-in-law. She is one of the strongest women I know; she lost her husband at a young age and raised five amazing children all on her own. I grew up across the street from her my entire life and got to observe her doing this (okay, my husband is literally the boy next door, or at least across the playground—yes it is a true love story). But I had one really small problem with her coming—she smoked and I had asthma.

Now how I responded to this dilemma is called 'third-party conflict' and we see it playing out in the workplace all the time. We take our conflict to the wrong person. Often it is the manager and we want them to 'fix' the other person for us. Now I teach this stuff, but often forget (perhaps I'm just practicing), so I turned to him in disbelief and said, "You are going to tell your mom not to smoke in the cabin, right? I could die, you know my asthma and all?" He looked at me with a sheepish chuckle and said, "Oh no, I'm not telling my mom not to smoke in the cabin, this is her domain. You know the rules—when she comes to our place she'll smoke outside, but in her home she gets to smoke."

I ask you, however, was I right, should she not have smoked in the cabin? Some of you will say yes, some no. The point I'm going to illustrate here is **"It doesn't matter if you are right; it only matters if you can find a third way.** This way of thinking is especially graceful if you can remember this when you are managing other people. It takes so much energy to prove you are right and I've seen people argue for hours or never speak to each other again because they are stuck on proving they are right and that the other person is wrong, instead of finding another way or a third way.

Velvet Hammer Technique #17
UNDERSTAND IT DOESN'T MATTER
IF YOU ARE RIGHT; IT ONLY MATTERS
IF YOU CAN FIND A THIRD WAY.

We got up to the cabin; she smoked outside all day, not one cigarette in the cabin. I was relieved, maybe she knew! Not telling someone diplomatically how you feel is usually called 'passive aggressive' behavior and sometimes it is a good option in a conflict, as long as you can let it go and not allow it to bother you anymore, to just accept it. Sometimes, however, it festers into something larger and it turns out not to have been the right choice to say nothing.

At around 9:00 p.m. we were still outside in our lawn chairs on this long hot summer day and, many of you will know, up north the mosquitoes come out about this time and we were forced to go inside the cabin. We played cards for about an hour. She didn't smoke. My husband was kicking me under the table, trying to indicate to me, "This is great, she knows, she isn't going to smoke inside." We all retired shortly after. My husband and the boys went down to a little hut with four bunk beds (where a couple of them smoked, too), and my daughter and I were offered the master bedroom and my mother-in-law took the back porch. She was wonderful and I couldn't have been more relieved that she did not smoke in the cabin and she was so thoughtful to give us the master bedroom.

I got into the 100-year-old roll-away bed, on which I put my own foamy, sheets, pillow and sleeping bag. I turned off the flashlight and played tag with one mosquito until about 1:00 a.m. I couldn't stand the smell of the old cabin and I couldn't sleep.

Around this time, I found out my mother-in-law had another bad habit; she was an insomniac. I heard her at the kitchen table, just outside my bedroom door, playing cards; I could hear the cards snapping. I lay there and waited. Sure enough, some time later I heard the click of the lighter and then a deep inhale and exhale. Now, how many of you don't smoke, and if someone smoked in the next room you'd know in an instant?

I grabbed the flashlight and checked the cracks

around the door and the smoke was wafting into my room. I grabbed towels and facecloths and began stuffing the door frame. It still came through. I got back into bed and tried to ignore it. I started to panic and used my inhaler several times. I lay there and counted the number of lighter clicks until about 5:00 a.m. when the sun came up. I wondered if my inhaler would last three more nights.

I finally realized I wouldn't be getting any sleep on this night and opened the door and asked with a wheezing voice, "Have you been smoking?" (in a very sheepish, passive-aggressive tone). She looked at me and said, "I've had one. Why, is the dog hair bothering you?" I was thinking, "Are you kidding me?" I smiled politely, took another wheezing breath and said, "I think so." (You guessed it.) She said, "Oh, don't worry, honey— we'll get that room washed down, bang out the carpet and get all that dog hair and dander out of the room. You'll be better tonight." I said nothing and just nodded okay. (I'd missed my chance.)

In the morning, who do you think got it? I nattered after my husband all day and said, "I can't believe you didn't say anything to your mother." He tried to calm me down and said it was only a couple more nights, he was sure I'd be fine. For three more days, with very little sleep and rationing my inhaler, I sat on the rocks by the water, swatting mosquitoes and watching everyone else having fun fishing, tubing, and jumping off the rocks into the freezing river. I realized I was a princess; I wanted a hair blower, a hot shower and a flush toilet more than anything else in the world.

BEWARE OF NEGATIVE IMPRINTING

On the drive home, I looked at my husband, still in disbelief that he couldn't see my side. I began to natter about the conflict again. Now, there is something else in conflict that you will want to be very aware of, it is called 'Negative Imprinting.' Negative imprinting is where you are in a conflict with someone and you are looking directly at their face, and are in an emotional state. For example, have you ever had a conflict with someone in your work and it was not resolved? You were angry and upset and looking at this person during the disagreement. After four or five of these incidents you've negatively imprinted their face into your brain. A phenomenon takes place. The person you are looking at 'takes on an ugly' appearance. They weren't ugly when you met them, but after four or five of these disagreements, you are having trouble sitting near them in a meeting. You begin to avoid them. You might even think, "Man, you weren't ugly when I met you, but now you're pretty ugly. In fact, I didn't even notice those nose hairs before."

Think about divorces; if you are in conflict all the time and looking at your significant other's face, after several years of this, you may wonder what you even saw in them in the first place. Beware of negative imprinting and to avoid this, I suggest grabbing a piece of paper that you can both look at to focus on resolving the conflict. I've given an example of what you can write on the paper in a few paragraphs. This way you are looking at the paper, not each other, to make sense of what the disagreement is about. You can get mad at the situation, not the person. Your anger or emotion is directed differently. If you can separate the person from the situation, you will be more successful at coming up with a resolution.

Velvet Hammer Technique #18
TO AVOID 'NEGATIVE IMPRINTING' GRAB A PIECE OF PAPER.

If I asked you to reflect on the last conflict you had, think about it—when was it and who was it with? Most people in my seminars say the following: my son, yesterday; my spouse, last night; my brother, last week; my boss, this morning; my colleague, three days ago. Isn't it amazing that most people don't say, "I think my last conflict was three years ago." This is because conflict is going to happen today, tomorrow next week, next year and the year after that. When do you think is the only time you'll ever get rid of conflict in your life? When you die! Some people say when you are sleeping, but I know some of you are having restless sleeps over conflicts. Would you like to know **the only thing that causes conflict,** whether it is at home, in your personal life or at your job or during your volunteer work?

Velvet Hammer Technique #19
THE ONLY THING THAT CAUSES CONFLICT IS WHEN YOUR GOALS, EXPECTATIONS OR OBJECTIVES ARE DIFFERENT FROM THE OTHER PERSON'S. FIND OUT WHAT EACH OTHER WANTS.

Every time there are differences there will be conflict. I've been teaching conflict resolution for years. A lot of it comes from my experience as a prison guard. My ability to handle the prison conflicts was a necessary skill, as my life often depended on it.

As we were driving home, and I was still nattering, my husband looked at me and said, "Okay, you teach this stuff. Grab the piece of paper." On a napkin in the car I wrote the following (and this is the template to use every time you get into a disagreement that you can't seem to instantly resolve):

I want	They want
No smoking	Smoke

Third way (to resolve this conflict):
(This is what we came up with in the car.)

- Bring a tent to sleep in

- Stay at the lodge up the river ($325 a night)

- Throw cigarettes in the river

- Sleep in the outhouse (she could have slept in the outhouse—it was a double seater, with room for a sleeping bag on the floor).

My mentor Barbara Colorosso, a speaker and author on child discipline, taught me something over 20 years ago when I had my first child and I was teaching behavior to children in the public school system that has stuck with me for years. Her quote was this: **"There is no problem so great that we can't solve it."** She feels that if we could teach this to our children and the people in our lives we could reduce the suicide rate by 50% in North America. Every time I get stuck in a conflict, I remember this quote and grab a piece of paper and write out the chart shown. Sometimes I come up with a third way or alternative right away and sometimes I need more time to contemplate it (even a day or so). I always ask myself, "Does it matter if you are right, or does it matter more that you find a resolution, a third way?" This thinking works well for most of the conflicts in which you will find yourself in your chosen work, volunteer or employment situation, and even your personal lives. Remember:

the only thing that is causing the conflict is that what the person wants is different from what you want. Identify that and you can go somewhere with it. Often people are so mad at the situation, they don't care what the other person wants, only what they want. Go ahead now and think of your last conflict; what did they want and what did you want? Is there an alternative to ensuring this doesn't arise again or to prevent it from happening in the future?

I want	They wanted

Third ways (to resolve this conflict):

•

•

•

As we went through these options, my husband looked at me in excitement. He said, "I've got the perfect answer—next year, don't come!" I looked at him in shock, and said, "Don't come? Why should I not come? I'm not even doing anything, she is the one blowing smoke!" I began to cry. I'd been kicked off the island and

I felt like I was in my own personal 'Survivor' television series. My tribe had sent me home. My husband looked at me with great care and concern and said, "Honey, I don't mean this in a mean way, but think about it—you hate it, you don't like the mosquitoes, you don't like the outhouse and you would prefer to have a blow dryer. If you don't like it, why do you come?" I stated, "Because it is my family vacation and I'm trying to support your love for this place." All of a sudden though, I had a brain swap. Have you ever been fighting for your position and all of a sudden you change your mind? I considered not going. Hmmm... I thought. I said, "You mean to tell me you would not be upset if I didn't go next year?" My husband said, "No, of course not. You really don't like it. I know it is uncomfortable for you. How about we go on our family vacation somewhere else and I'll bring the kids up with their grandmother on my own for a few days each year?" I'm telling you, if I could have gotten out on the highway and done a skippy dance at that moment, I would have. Don't go! It was perfect. So now each year we try to go on a family vacation with a chandelier in the lobby and a flush toilet, and he gets to go to the cabin. We found our third way.

Now I ask you again, was I right? Should she have not smoked in the cabin? The point is, and I'll state it again, it doesn't matter if you are right, it only matters if you can find a third way. I saw a stress doctor once who said, "Do you want to be right, or do you want to be happy?" Finding alternatives, third ways, options after you've declared what each other's wants or needs are, is one of the greatest ways to overcome even seemingly impossible conflicts.

RESOLVING THIRD-PARTY CONFLICTS

If you have two people on your team involved in a conflict, you can guide them through this process. Let them know the only thing that is causing the conflict is that their wants, expectations or objectives are different from each other's. Don't take sides. Grab a piece of paper, draw the chart, identify the different needs and start asking them what else they could do to find a third way or a resolution so this does not happen in the future. I often don't add my suggestion until many ideas are on the list. If I don't think any of the solutions will work, I say, "What else?" and keep going. If we can't come up with something, I ask everyone to think about it and get back to me with an idea by end of the next day.

Velvet Hammers always move to the side of resolutions and are solution-focused instead of being blame-focused. This will make you a stronger leader. Don't get trapped in a contest of wills. Remember the quote from Barbara Colorosso, "There is no problem so great we can't solve it." There will always be mistakes; most people don't make them intentionally. If a lot of negative imprinting has gone on, they may have the wrong intentions, and this is where resolutions need to be found— quickly. If I see myself involved in negative imprinting, this is my cue to go for coffee and talk it out when calm heads can prevail. Maintain open communication; when people are no longer in an emotional state you can break the negative cycle.

Velvet Hammers also know how to stand their ground with "the bully in the backyard" and how to tell someone to "Knock it off" nicely, so people can keep their self esteem intact. Velvet Hammers still bring issues to the table but they find out the reasons people don't perform up to standard and find ways to correct it. In the next chapter we'll also discuss the stages of discipline and what to do with someone on your team who refuses to live up to the obligations of the job.

CHAPTER 7

The Bully in the Backyard

DISCIPLINE & DEVELOPMENT

WHAT DISCIPLINE MEANS

Strong leaders build people up—
they don't take them out

WHEN someone is performing or behaving poorly it can create havoc in the team and damage the team's ability to meet goals. If this conduct is accepted or ignored by the leader, the standards are lowered by everyone. The other team members ask, "If one person does not have to do it, why should I?" Due to the need for inclusion, sometimes women find disciplinary or reprimanding conversations difficult. They can find it challenging to single someone out and delay having the conversation until it is too late or the problem explodes. They sometimes ignore it completely, believing it to be petty. If nothing is said to someone who is creating havoc or performing poorly, the rest of the team is flabbergasted and frustrated, as someone not pulling their weight usually affects their performance as well. Discipline is often a gift to you, your team and the person who is not performing up to standard.

If you think of the root word of 'discipline,' which is *disciple*, the word means "to teach." If we approach discipline from this angle, in other words to prop someone up vs. taking them out, discipline becomes much easier. Be the guide, coach or teacher when you discipline someone; this intent is always 'softer' than direct punishment (unless you have to, which we discuss later when someone won't do a task that is critical to the success of the team). In most cases you won't get the same level of defensiveness when you use this approach. Your job as a leader is not necessarily to be liked, but to develop people into the best they can be and make people productive. The team expects you to do this, fairly and gracefully. This chapter shows you some skills and Velvet Hammer techniques when disciplining others.

HANDLING THE BULLY IN THE BACKYARD

One of the toughest situations to handle is someone who blatantly takes you on in front of other people. In other words, publicly humiliates you, puts you down or visibly disagrees. It is an awkward situation and one that must be handled well. When—or if—this occurs, if you would like to hold on to any respect and credibility as a leader, it should be handled well. Everyone is watching you and expecting you to handle it like a pro.

One of my first challenges in the corporate world as a manager occurred directly after a merger in the airline industry. Now, anyone who has been through a merger knows that a lot of people aren't happy. Change is hard on everyone, and we often feel that the change is wrong. Because "we didn't do it that way," people code it as being "wrong." Then they get upset.

The first day after the merger in the airline industry, I put on my new uniform to do a performance review on a person who in essence had done my job the day before, only the 'in-charge' position at the new airline by which we'd just been purchased was a union job. The only real difference between me and him (besides years of experience) was that with the old airline I had come from, the 'in-charge' position on each flight had the ability to hire, fire and suspend employees. This employee at the other airline of whom I was to do the performance review did not.

This 'in-charge' employee was quite senior to me; in fact, I believe he was a veteran of 20-plus years. I had approximately four years in the industry at this time. When I showed up and introduced myself, I knew it was going to be a rough day; as I introduced myself he walked away.

The flight began; it was a quick day with a few stops. On the first leg of the journey I decided to sit down in a passenger seat and stay out of the way. The last row, aisle seat was empty so I observed from there. The only problem was that the reading light was out. It was in the days when a full hot breakfast was served and it was a full flight. I waited until most of the dishes were away and we started to land. I then went up the aisle and when

I got to the front galley, where the 'in-charge' was busy putting the last items away, I handed him a piece of paper that said, "Reading light burned 24D."

This was a simple request where the person in charge of the cabin normally would log it in the maintenance book so that at the station stop a maintenance person would pop in a new light bulb, so the next person would not have a reading light that was burned out.

I guess he felt this was the wrong time, because in front of two crew members and within earshot of about the first six rows, he screamed at me, "What are you, an idiot? Can't you see we are landing? Get out of my way!" Now, I ask you for a moment to reflect. What would you have done? If you state right there, "Wait a minute, you can't speak to me like that, I am your manager and that is insubordination in front of everyone," you will lose. It is not the time to come to the fight. On the other hand, if you say, "I'm sorry, I didn't mean to bother you at this time," you will lose overwhelmingly. One thing I learned when working at the prison was that when someone screamed, or swore, or threatened you, you did not come to the fight. Delay it until you can deal with it, unless it is an emergency situation.

Velvet Hammer Technique #20
DON'T COME TO THE FIGHT—DELAY IT UNTIL YOU CAN DEAL WITH IT APPROPRIATELY.

Those of you in emergency services such as medical, police or ambulance, will often not have the luxury to delay dealing with the issue. Someone has to make a decision and this technique might not be an option. What I said in this particular situation, and have used numerous other times, works quite well, "I see you are upset; we'll talk about it after." Neither agree, nor disagree. Acknowledge the disapproval or disagreement of the person, and delay a confrontation until you can tackle the issue privately. This statement neutralizes the situation. You may alter it to "I see this is a challenge; we'll speak after." But the point is to get out of the public humiliation without losing your cool, while not indicating that the behavior is appropriate.

Often if someone disagrees with me in a meeting and their frustration is not shared by the rest of the team, I take it offline by acknowledging that the person finds the situation challenging, and ask them to discuss it after the meeting. I'm not going to let them 'suck me in' to a fight I'm not prepared for, nor a fight that should not be publicly aired. Your team will be happy you didn't and you will save face.

These types of situations usually occur because the person is upset due to certain expectations not being met, or they've got other issues in their personal life (money, marriage, kids) and in this case 'the merger.' I'm sure he felt, "How does this person feel they have the right to critique my work when they've only had a few years' experience?"

A negative attitude can be quickly established when an individual's expectations are not met, and you might not even have anything directly to do with it, but you are in the line of fire. Get out of it with grace and eloquence, gain respect and keep your credibility. Don't come to the fight; delay it until you can.

There were repercussions from the incident and we did get the chance to sort things out in a formal meeting the next day, including our feelings about the merger. This situation could have turned out differently had I not delayed the fight until two people could talk with calm heads; there would have been the paperwork for insubordination, grievance hearings and a lot of additional effort. The paperwork to enforce a suspension, when someone was just frustrated with change, was not worth the effort to me in this case. He should not have behaved that way, but I'd rather find a different way to ensure the situation wouldn't happen again if I could.

I do believe that sometimes you will move to progressive discipline, but do it privately and do it when there is no other recourse, which I discuss in Chapter 8. Being able to communicate with a hothead or bully without being anxious or intimidated is a great skill a strong leader can exhibit.

WHY PEOPLE PERFORM POORLY

Why do people perform poorly? There are generally four reasons people's performance is substandard.

1. Didn't Know or Understand

The first reason is that they didn't know. Now you may say, "Geesh, I told them this morning." But something I always remember, when I was taught communication skills years ago, that has stuck with me for a lifetime is, "It does not matter what you say, it only matters what gets heard."

To illustrate this point, in my seminars I tell people I live in the Tri-Cities and then tell them the names of the three cities. By lunch time, I ask them, who can tell me the names of the Tri-Cities. At the time of writing this, I've not had one person recall them exactly (unless of course, I'm training in my own hometown). I then state, "Geesh, I just told you this morning." Have you ever told someone something and hours later they say, "You didn't say that, or you never told me?"

Maybe the words were said, but they have been misinterpreted, or the employee was busy with something else, or what you said was complex and they only remembered a portion of it. A person will only listen if they have the capacity to hear (they are focused on what you are saying and are not doing something else) and the willingness to listen (they are not upset or angry about the subject).

Another reason people say they "didn't know" is because the expectation has not been consistently enforced. They may mean, "I **didn't know you really meant it.**" This is especially true if you've said it but never really followed up on it, or you've said it but let people get away with not conforming to a rule. Think about when someone is late, do you say something consistently, or have you let it slide? If you let things go frequently, especially on the important things (think goals from the previous chapter), people will also never really know what you want or expect.

Another challenge in 'didn't know' is they may never have been trained, or at least not trained properly. They may not have been taught the way you prefer things, especially if you are a new supervisor or manager taking over from someone else. This can be frustrating for the employee because they may not know "why" you want it different and protest silently, by saying, "We don't do it that way." Change is hard.

I always give the person the benefit of the doubt. When I get frustrated with the way someone is doing something I remember my belief that: "There are no stupid people in life, only people with skill gaps." You may chuckle, but you won't believe how many times I have to say that to myself at grocery lineups and car rental and airline counters. I give them the benefit of the doubt when I'm not getting what I'm expecting and turn into the teacher. I always try to re-phrase my statements with a question, then turn to offer a suggestion (think 'teach').

Velvet Hammer Technique #21
THERE ARE NO STUPID PEOPLE, JUST PEOPLE WITH SKILL GAPS. TURN INTO THE TEACHER.

2. Aptitude Issues

Another reason people perform poorly is because of aptitude; it doesn't matter how much training you give them, they just are not suitable for that particular task. Think about Chapter 2, where we reviewed personality styles. Some individuals with extreme personality traits find it very difficult to alter or adapt. Some people are more suited to detailed work, others to working with people. Another problem may be a learning disability that either the employee has never identified, or he or she may be too self-conscious to inform you about. A percentage of the population cannot read, and a certain percentage struggles with the written word. Be careful if you are giving written instructions via manuals or emails to individuals you suspect may have this kind of difficulty.

3. Not Permitted To

Yet another challenge is *expecting* someone to do a task or take the initiative. They are unsure if they truly have the authority to do it and are too embarrassed to ask or bring it to someone's attention, as they don't want to look like they are questioning authority or are stupid. Here is an example to illustrate this point: an executive assistant who reported to several vice-presidents had to send out all letters and documentation given to her within a 24-hour period. The problem was that two of the VPs would not permit her to send out the correspondence without their signatures. What would she do if they were out in the field for two days? Without fully investigating, the office manager fired her for not meeting the expectations of the job. She won her case in court, as the organization had not fully investigated why she was not meeting the requirement. This only came to light when they heard her defending her reasoning in court in her own words, and they realized they should have asked her directly why she couldn't meet the job requirements. Try to find out why someone isn't meeting the job standards. Don't let a judge find out, unless you have to or the person refuses to tell you.

Another example of 'not being permitted to' is equipment breaking down, such as photocopiers, phone systems, computers, etc. Also, systemic problems can create havoc, like procedures, incorrect forms or information and policies that inflict across-the-board challenges for customers and people working for the organization. In these situations, people can't possibly meet deadlines or production schedules. When a manager finds that an employee is not performing well, it is the manager's job to find out why the employee is not or cannot meet the requirements and find ways to help them get there. I don't allow excuses, because things do break; there are always systemic breakdowns. I always ask for work-arounds for both the individual and the bigger teams. It is important for people to be solution-oriented during these types of situations. It does not matter what organization or team you are leading, one thing I can guarantee you is that things will not always go as planned.

4. Will Not Do it

The last example is where an employee feels this is not their job and simply won't do it or has an attitude and just won't do it. It is the hardest one to manage and often requires stronger disciplinary steps, which I'll explain in a moment. This situation can be caused by anger or emotional upset, union contractual interpretations (ensure both of you are clear in your respective interpretations) or even laziness or boredom. When it is a poor attitude you will recognize it right away because of rolling of eyes, folded arms, or them telling you directly. They may say they will do it to your face, but turn around and just not do it. They'll even go to the water cooler with their colleagues and say, "I'm not going to do it, are you going to do it?" right after telling you, "Okay." or "Yes, no problem." If you are familiar with supervising people you may have seen this take place. Unfortunately you don't even know this is going on until you find out that no one is doing the requested task.

Taking Disciplinary Action

Investigate the situation by asking questions of the person. The few key questions I use and start with are why, where, who and what? to find out why they are not meeting expectations. For example:

1. Why did you think that?
2. Where did you get that information or idea?
3. Who advised you or told you that? (be careful here—you are not looking to blame anyone)
4. What was the reason you felt that way?

Based on their answers I can usually determine if it is a 'Didn't Know,' an 'Aptitude Issue,' 'Not Permitted To' or just plain 'Won't Do It'. Let's review what to do once you've determined what you are dealing with.

What to do if it is a 'Didn't Know'

a) Offer further training.

b) Make expectations clear (and follow up in writing)

What to do if it is an 'Aptitude Issue'

a) Change tasks to match aptitude.

b) Offer further training until it is a confirmed aptitude issue.

c) Transfer to a position that is more suitable, in which they can succeed.

d) Last resort—you may have to terminate.

What to do if it is a 'Not Permitted'

a) Give or support them to get the authority or permission if you can, if not take away that responsibility.

b) Remove obstacles or find work-arounds.

c) Change deadlines or production schedules to accommodate equipment failures, etc.

DISCIPLINE AND DEVELOPMENT

What to do if it is a 'Won't Do It'

In this situation you will have to move forward with what is often known as progressive discipline. The four stages are as follows:

1. Verbal Warning (discussion)
2. Letter of Warning
3. Suspension or leave of absence
4. Termination

In Chapter 8 I will take you through these steps in detail as your final options. We will also look at a technique I call 'Knock It Off Nicely,' so that you can bring things to people's attention quickly and without apprehension or anxiety. If you were doing something wrong or making someone angry, would not like to know? You owe it to them and you owe it to yourself to bring things to people's attention.

CHAPTER 8

Knock It Off Nicely

REPRIMANDS AND FINAL OPTIONS

CORRECTING PERFORMANCE ISSUES

TO tell someone that their performance is sub-standard or that they are doing something wrong can feel awkward or like a personal attack. And when the information is not communicated properly it can feel like a personal attack. Outlined below is a technique that works exceptionally well because we tell someone that their conduct or behavior is inappropriate by not using the word "you" in our opening dialogue. When we remove the word "you," it focuses on the situation, the problem or challenge rather than the person, enabling us to neutralize the situation.

Once I became good at it, I could use this technique to reprimand employees, volunteers and even my boss or my father without them knowing I had just reprimanded them. Additionally, I could do it publicly, on airplanes for instance, where we didn't have an office or private place to go to. It also forms the basis for progressive discipline and the documentation you will have to prepare.

The technique looks like this: think of a person on your team who is not performing to standard or something you would like corrected. Fill in the blanks here.

Photocopy the pages you will need or go to
www.thevelvethammer.com
to download the 'Knock It Off Nicely' outlines.

THE KNOCK IT OFF NICELY TECHNIQUE

Velvet Hammer Technique #22
THINK CONDUCT, IMPACT, FIXED!

Step 1 – Conduct or Behavior

Describe in detail the conduct or behavior they are exhibiting that needs to be corrected. Examples include error rate high, not wearing safety shoes, chewing gum, missing deadlines, personal phone calls or surfing the net excessively for personal use. This technique can even be used for bad breath or body odor in a customer service situation, low necklines, short skirts or even very sensitive and personal issues that have to be addressed. Be careful to describe it specifically; it is not specific enough to say the behavior is a negative attitude, as you may face a backlash and the person could disagree with you. If it is a negative attitude that you are dealing with, be specific. Examples include slamming phones, folding arms across the chest, rolling the eyes. On the lines below, describe specifically the behavior the person is exhibiting.

Photocopy this page.

Conduct or Behavior (that needs correcting)

_____

_____

_____

_____

Step 2 – Impact of the Conduct or Behavior

You must explain to someone 'why' the conduct or behavior is impacting the organization, team or objectives, otherwise the mention of the conduct or behavior can be deemed 'petty.' If you ever do proceed through to the termination of an employee, during a wrongful dismissal case the judge will want to know how it affected the business. Often individuals don't take the time to look at how their conduct is preventing or limiting their work in some way. List the impacts of the behavior, for example:

> **Conduct:** *Missing deadlines.* **Impact:** Cost overruns, loss of customers, holding up other departments or team members.
>
> **Conduct:** *Error rate high.* **Impact:** Rework, loss of customers, lost productivity, missed deadlines, financial loss.
>
> **Conduct:** *Chewing gum.* **Impact:** Loss of customers due to perception of professionalism, distracting to others.
>
> **Conduct:** *Bad breath.* **Impact:** Loss of customers, lost sales.
>
> **Conduct:** *Excessive personal phone calls or surfing net.* **Impact:** Lost productivity, missed deadlines, can place additional burden on other team members who have to complete work.

On the following lines, describe specifically the impact of the conduct or behavior you have noted.

Photocopy this page.

Impact (impact of the behavior or conduct you listed previously)

Step 3 – Describe what it would look like if it was fixed.
If you miss this step, you can slip into a 'didn't know' situation. The individual might say, "You never told me how to fix it, you just said you didn't like it." Alternatively, if you miss this step, they could make it up or have their own interpretation of how they should fix it. For some things it is quite obvious, for instance you want the conduct immediately stopped, discontinued or eliminated. If you are applying this technique in progressive discipline, you'll want to document this clearly. The judge during a wrongful dismissal case will want to see that you instructed (developed) the employee by telling them *what* to do, not just *what not* to do. Sometimes it feels like the same thing and you seem to be 'book ending' the discussion and repeating yourself, but that is okay—it reinforces your expectations. For example:

Conduct: *Missing deadlines.* **Impact:** Cost overruns, loss of customers, holding up other departments or team members. **Fixed:** concerted effort to meet deadlines and sufficient notice when a deadline can't be met and why, in order to see if there is another workaround.

Conduct: *Error rate high.* **Impact:** Rework, loss of customers, lost productivity, missed deadlines, financial loss. **Fixed:** an effort to check work, or bring to our attention what further training might be required to minimize the frequency of the errors.

Conduct: *Chewing gum.* **Impact:** Loss of customers due to perception of professionalism, distracting to others **Fixed:** an immediate and discontinued use of chewing gum when in front of customers.

Conduct: *Bad breath.* **Impact:** Loss of customers, lost sales. **Fixed:** the elimination of eating spicy or strong foods prior to coming to work or the ongoing use of breath mints.

Conduct: *Excessive phone calls or surfing net for personal use.* **Impact:** Lost productivity and missed deadlines can cause additional burden on other team members who have to complete work. **Fixed:** save phone calls and internet surfing for personal use during assigned breaks.

On the following lines, describe specifically what it would look like if it was fixed or corrected.

Photocopy this page.

What it would like if it was fixed or corrected; think *teaching* or *developing*:

_____

_____

_____

_____

_____

_____

_____

_____

_____

_____

_____

_____

Here is the framework for the script that you can use over and over again to begin a conversation to correct conduct or behavior. All you have to do is fill in the blanks. Feel free to alter it to make it comfortable for you. The main rule for this technique is *not* to use the word "you" in your opening statement when bringing something to the attention of the individual. Following this framework will keep you from apologizing or getting sidetracked. When someone wants to pull you into their problems, you can always resort to this statement, stating that you understand the way they feel, but you still need this to be corrected in the future.

THE KNOCK IT OFF NICELY SCRIPT

The Velvet Hammer Technique #23
WHEN CRITICIZING SOMEONE
DON'T USE THE WORD "YOU."

By identifying the conduct, its impact and what it would look like if it was corrected, you are ready to fill in the blanks. It is like a 'paint by numbers' script for disciplining and correcting performance, and it works.

Here is the script:

When someone does _____(conduct), the impact is _____, _____, _____ (impact). **What I need to see is** _____ (fixed or corrected).

Photocopy this page.

For instance,

You are with an employee who has been demonstrating a negative attitude. Here is an example of what to say, using the framework and script discussed:

(**Conduct**) When someone rolls their eyes and folds their arms in meetings, (**Impact**) other team members can be discouraged from bringing ideas to the table.

Possible solutions or other options to problems or challenges often don't get discussed and we miss an opportunity to fix things. (**Corrected or Fixed**) If there is a problem that is frustrating, what I need to see is that possible solutions or ideas are brought forward, or a request is made for such a discussion to take place.

Do not speak right away. Wait a moment for a response. Now, many people in my seminar ask, "Yes, but since I did not use 'you,' what if they don't know I'm talking about them?" In most cases the person will know you are speaking about them. And we have not finished the conversation yet, this statement is just the first three sentences to start it off. Now we must provide 'proof,' so the manager will have examples of when the conduct has been exhibited. Often they can be used as teaching tools to identify where things might be off track. For example, the leader may now say, "For instance, last Tuesday in the meeting when the changes to the reports were announced, (now you can use "you") you folded your arms, rolled your eyes and would not make any eye contact. This can be perceived as negative and can create uneasiness amongst the team."

Practice these types of statements with someone. Often people in the seminars slip out and use the word "you." You might find it a very hard habit to break. I recommend you practice it (especially for the sensitive issues or with a strong personality) so you can get comfortable not using the word "you" in your statements.

Step 1 —Verbal Warning

This is an example of step 1 in the progressive discipline process. The framework of these *knock it off nicely* statements can be used for a verbal warning and create the premise for all other documentation. As mentioned, a judge in a wrongful dismissal case will want to know:

a) Did you tell the employee specifically what **conduct** was hindering the job requirements?
b) Did you tell the employee the **impact** of their actions or lack of action?
c) Did you tell the employee what it would look like if it was **fixed**? (development/training)

Often just the conversation will correct the conduct. If the situation is serious enough, or you believe it will be repeated, document that the conversation took place by sending an email or letter. The email might sound something like this (remember, if you have a collective agreement and work in a union environment, check the contract and check with your experts if you are unsure):

Thank you for taking the time today to discuss the importance of bringing ideas and suggestions to the table when frustrating situations occur. As mentioned, certain body language can be deemed negative and squash possible resolutions from others. I look forward to your continued support.

Remember, don't put anything in an email that you don't want on the 6:00 p.m. news. If employees are disgruntled enough they can share it around. Also, don't ever send one when you are angry. Save it, review it and edit it if you have to. Remember, the intent is to develop people.

Record or document The good news is that you have recorded the date in your email, given them a notification, and you will have a permanent record that the conversation has taken place. Keep this in your files in the event you may have to move to the next step in progressive discipline. Nothing typically goes into the personnel file of the employee at this time, unless this is your policy. Always check with Human Resources or a lawyer when you move into progressive discipline if you are unsure. Remember, the intent of the letter should be to prop people up, not take them out. In the next step of progressive discipline the tone can become serious.

Step 2 – Letter of Warning

The next step is the letter of warning. Typically, if it is *not for the same conduct,* you can't proceed to stage 2 (again, check with your experts on the policies). If it is now tardiness (being late), you will usually have to go back to stage 1, a verbal warning. It takes some time to actually terminate someone, and this is one of the reasons that hiring smartly upfront is so important, to ensure you don't get into issues later. You also have to ensure that if the person has made moves to correct their conduct, you have documented this as well, otherwise it can be deemed a 'witch hunt'. Remember that company theft or other harmful or dangerous behavior a person exhibits can justify an automatic termination; you might not have to go through the four stages of progressive discipline.

The letter of warning should be easy, since you've already had the conversation once. You would use the same script but it would sound something like this (using your earlier email as a reference):

On xyz date, we discussed the importance of bringing suggestions and ideas forward during situations you found frustrating (as the subject has already been brought to their attention previously, you can use "you"). *Yesterday during the meeting when we were discussing report finalization, you slammed down your pen, folded your arms and didn't speak for the duration of the meeting. What I need to see is an immediate discontinuation of these behaviors in meetings. Again, if there is a situation you find frustrating, please bring it to my attention after the meeting so that, in the event that you don't have an immediate idea or alternative as to what you deem to be a problem, we don't squash other ideas. Failure to do so will result in further disciplinary action.*

Document   The letter of warning is documented something like this:

On xyz date it was brought to your attention that conduct such as slamming pens, folding arms and rolling the eyes does not offer a supportive environment for idea sharing. The behaviors exhibited can intimidate other team members and therefore possible solutions are not brought forward and the organization can be limited in progressing with alternative approaches and product innovation. It is expected that this conduct cease immediately. Failure to do so will result in further disciplinary action.

A copy goes to the employee, one goes in your file for your records and one goes in the employee's personnel file. The next manager of the department, should you move on or leave, can pull out the employee file and see that the first **two** stages have been completed and they are documented. They don't have to start back at stage 1. When things have not been documented, it is one of the biggest frustrations for organizations and managers. Often poor performers hang on for years and managers move on or leave and insufficient documentation is on file.

Step 3 – Suspension or Leave of Absence

Whenever you remove income from an individual, ensure you check with your experts. This is where it can get tricky. A suspension or leave of absence can be done with or without pay and can last typically from one day to three. If it is for an absentee problem, I would probably not offer pay. The actual intent of a suspension is not for punishment but to give an employee the time to reflect and consider if they are willing or able to meet the requirements of the job.

This conversation should be even easier and swifter as it has already taken place twice. With suspensions I always ask another manager to join me as a witness. Ask the other manager not to speak and to stay neutral in the meeting. It should be quick. The conversation may go like this:

On xyz date and again today, it was brought to your attention the importance of bringing suggestions and ideas forward during situations you find frustrating. Yesterday during the meeting when we were discussing product ideas, you didn't speak or participate and left the room in haste before the meeting was over. We've asked that this type of conduct and outbursts be discontinued and that frustrations are dealt with privately. This behavior cannot continue and we are going to suspend you without pay for a period of two days. Upon your return we will discuss possible options, alternatives and/or further training.

Document   The suspension letter would look something like the one below (again, review with the experts). A copy goes to the employee, one goes into your file for your records and one goes into the employee's personnel file. The next manager of the department, should you move on or leave, can pull out the employee file and see that the first **three** stages have been completed and they are documented.

On xyz date, another xyz date and again today, we have determined that the expected performance standards outlined in previous documentation have not been adhered to. An outburst yesterday resulted in the early cancellation of a meeting and productivity was once again impaired. We are requesting that you take this time to reflect and review whether you will be able to meet the job expectations as outlined previously, and report to us with your comments and ideas on how this situation may be corrected. This suspension will occur from _____date/time to _____date/time. Please report back to: _____(location) at _____(time) on _____date. Failure to do so may result in further disciplinary action.

You will want to leave room for signatures. Ensure you obtain your own signature, the witness's signature and the employee's. If the employee refuses to sign, then note this on the document and your witness can sign and confirm.

Sometimes the employee goes on their leave, sees the writing on the wall and seeks alternative employment. Occasionally they don't return after their suspension. If they do report back at the requested time, with your witness present, proceed by asking the employee if they feel they can meet the requirements and performance expectations of the job. Note how they answer. You should also ask if there are any other suggestions they have that would help them meet the performance requirements.

These measures may include further training or a transfer to another role or position. It is always necessary to get feedback from the employee. Sometimes the employee is requested to put their comments, needs or ideas into a letter for their file. Sometimes the employee is unresponsive or demonstrates anger. Remember, don't come to the fight, stay neutral and professional. Go back to the framework: conduct, its impact, and what you need to see, so you don't get sidetracked. Remember, through all the stages of progressive discipline you are seeking ways to keep the employee employed and developed. Sometimes, however, the person does not fit the job and it is best that they move on.

Documentation Prepare written documentation that states and confirms the outcomes of this meeting. Use the same framework as in previous documentation, but also list the outcomes or actions to which both the employee and the employer have agreed. For instance, the employee has agreed to fully engage in meetings and discontinue disruptive behaviors. The employer has agreed to provide conflict-resolution training.

Step 4 – Termination

This is often the most challenging time for a manager or supervisor. The employee may have slipped back into old habits. In my seminars managers often ask, "How many times do I have to tell them?" Well, four times for sure, and these had better be documented. You wonder why people don't change; let me ask you this—have you ever seen anyone try to change a behavior such as smoking, losing weight or biting their nails? These are ingrained behaviors that have been learned and imprinted. It is very hard for people to change. And guess what—you can't change anyone. The only thing you can do is provide some motivation for them to change themselves. Either a reward or a consequence is the only thing you can offer. The rest is up to them. You will never change another person. Only they can decide that.

The Velvet Hammer Technique #24
YOU WILL NEVER CHANGE ANOTHER PERSON. AS A LEADER YOU CAN ONLY PROVIDE A REWARD OR A CONSEQUENCE AND THEN THE INDIVIDUAL DECIDES WHAT ACTION THEY WILL TAKE.

So here you are, after several months the employee reverts to the conduct that you have brought to their attention. The day before in a meeting, they have again struck out verbally at another individual. It is time to take the necessary action.

A few tips on termination:

a) Avoid terminating on a Friday. The employee often has the entire weekend to fret about the situation. They can become either depressed or begin to rant. Over the weekend, without anything productive to do about the situation, they can start speaking to people who—instead of encouraging them to take positive actions such as getting another job, moving on or learning from the situation—tell them to sue.

b) If you can do it at the end of the day, call them into your office five minutes before closing. This way the employee can clean out their desk or locker and can avoid the humiliation of being sent home in front of their peers.

c) Sometimes the termination is done offsite in case a heated discussion or altercation occurs. This course of action would prevent other team members witnessing an event that may disturb them.

d) When a termination has occurred it is wise for the manager to be very brief about the situation to the team. A comment that _____(name of individual) has moved on to seek other employment is all that needs to be said. Do not under any circumstances discuss the situation or events with the team. In doing so you may jeopardize a wrongful dismissal case if one ensues. If someone pressures you, state that it is confidential and you are unable to discuss any details.

Bring the employee in and state the dates on which the problem has been brought to their attention. Explain very briefly, for example:

"Unfortunately you have not been able to meet the requirements and expectations of this position. You are therefore terminated from employment at _____."

Offer any further instructions about paperwork, cleaning out their desk, etc.

Sometimes you may want to wish them success in an area for which they may be better suited. From time to time, an escort will be required to ensure they do not remove anything that does not belong to them. In some cases your Human Resources department will help you with any further logistics such as the retrieval of building keys, corporate identification, phone lines or voice mail, email configuration, etc. Otherwise you will have to ensure you've covered all aspects of the termination yourself.

Documentation   The letter should be drafted and presented either at the meeting or delivered the next day. Basically it should follow the same framework, stating the conduct and the impact and what you were hoping to see if it was fixed. Note the dates of the other three stages of it being brought to their attention. You may wish to close with a statement that wishes them success in finding future employment more suitable to their talents. **Again, I cannot stress enough that you obtain guidance and expert opinions throughout the progressive discipline stages. They will ensure you are following labor standards for your region, state, province or country.**

It is not as hard as it seems, as long as you have both the skill and tenacity to handle the issue well and a framework from which to work. When disciplining, one of the biggest hurdles is worrying that the person will be upset. They might be, but you have an issue to correct; it is an obligation of being in a leadership role.

CHAPTER 9

The Day I Stabbed the Turkey

DON'T GET IT ALL DONE—GET HELP

Are we fooling ourselves? I'm sure I'll finish in first place—next year!

AS I write this chapter I've just taken a lemon meringue pie out of the oven, the spaghetti sauce is in the crock pot for later tonight, I've started a load of laundry, finished the grocery shopping, sent out 3 emails and written two cheques. Now I can start to think about my work; it is 9:00 a.m. I still feel no further ahead than yesterday. Does this sound like one of your typical days? If you step into a leadership role, not only do you already have additional personal responsibilities, but you also have more people counting on you. Your areas of accountability increase and everyone starts demanding your time, often as soon as you walk in the door. How does one balance it all? You don't—you get help!

I learned this Velvet Hammer technique one Christmas, which is what we celebrate in our home, but I'm sure you know how hectic things can get no matter what holidays you celebrate. Yes, as mentioned in Chapter 1, I had managed to prepare the many wonderful intricacies of a Martha Stewart seasonal holiday (okay, I'm exaggerating—I'm not too good at all the fussy stuff, but I didn't do too badly). The house was decorated, the packages had been wrapped and torn open, the scented candles were burning, the tree was twinkling with lights and the Christmas carols that had been playing all day were now starting to wear thin. The turkey, which was a little overdone, was being pulled out of the oven, the gravy was burning, the vegetables boiling over and everyone was running around or doing their own thing. My hair was stuck flat to my forehead with sweat, the lovely dress I'd put on was stained with cranberry sauce, and my oven mitts had a big hole in them, so I burned my finger.

At the moment of truth, when the turkey was to be carved and the gravy strained, my husband picked up the phone to call his relatives back east. He'd forgotten to phone them all day and with the time difference didn't want to call too late. He thought this moment was the 'right' time; I thought differently. As he cheerfully chatted to his brother, he turned his back to me as I frantically waved the electric carving knife over my head to indicate that this was not the time. I could not believe he was going to delay this almost perfectly timed dinner to talk on the phone. In absolute frustration (and a little disbelief), I drove the electric knife into the bird and ran upstairs crying. Everything felt ruined.

Have you ever felt like this? Overwhelmed and no one comes to your aid? They all looked at me like I was the lunatic and I was thinking, "Who do you think I am, the maid?"

Velvet Hammer Technique #25
DON'T GET IT ALL DONE—GET HELP.

One has to remember, as mentioned earlier in the book, that women are amazing multi-taskers and we can often get it all done, but then there can be nothing left to give at the moment we need it most. The situation I just described to you was such a bolt of lightning for me. I asked if it was my fault I was feeling this way; I never asked for help. If I'd mentioned that I needed help, my family would have jumped in to help me. Okay, my daughter may have grumbled a little at first, but she would have done it.

Also, one year ago a life-changing event occurred, which I would call another bolt of lightning. I was diagnosed with Multiple Sclerosis, a neurological disease that is gradually degenerative and at the time of writing this book, there is no cure. I'm doing well right now; I just have pins and needles in my hands so far, but I am more conscious of what I will do and won't do.

I've always been a busy person—I think it comes from my grandmother—but this was my wake-up call. This is what really made me understand, 'don't get it all done—get help.' One of the symptoms made it difficult for me to put my hands in hot water. That meant I couldn't even do the dishes or wash the bathtubs. So finally I broke down and hired a housekeeper. She comes in once every two weeks and does an amazing job. If you have never considered this and you feel you are over-whelmed, give yourself a gift.

I told myself for years that I couldn't hire a house-keeper, that I couldn't afford it. I can clean my sinks and shine my taps as good as someone else. When I finally realized the burden this removed for me and saw my weekends open up, I could not believe I had waited so long. To afford this expense we stopped going out for dinner on that week. It paid for 3 hours of housekeeping. Search around; often there are many affordable options for housekeeping. This might not be an issue for you, but when you are managing people at work and trying to get it all done at home, you will burn out and often become resentful towards everyone else; save yourself the grief if you feel this might help.

Keep delegating in other areas of your life. Another thing I believe in is, if you have children, give them as much responsibility as early as possible. My daughter started grade four this year, she is nine years old at the time of writing this book. In the last 3 days, I've taught her how to set her alarm, select and lay out the clothes she wants to wear to school the night before and how to pack her lunch. She was excited as we went through how to pack a healthy lunch. She loves it, because she gets to decide what is going in her lunch and she gets to eat what she feels like (within reason), and this is where I'm there to offer guidance only. Delegate at work and delegate at home.

Other Time-Saving Tips
If you want some time-saving tips, here is what I do:

1. Close your email down while at your computer and check it at set intervals. I've found answering email as soon as I get it eats away 10 minutes here and 10 minutes there, adding up to a quick hour when I have a deadline or something looming.
2. Make important phone calls first thing in the morning. This way, people have all day to get back to you.
3. When you have to wait for appointments, always take your reading material that you wanted to get through.
4. If you have touched a document, file it right away. Clutter is my worst enemy and I still fight it.
5. Keep only those things you are using on your desktop or work area, everything else file or put away.
6. If you have to get something done, but you want to keep an open-door policy, put up a sign for times when you absolutely need to get something done, or go to an empty boardroom or office (even a local coffee shop), but let people know where and why you are going.
7. If someone is taking up too much of your time ask them to reconvene and pick a time. If you don't nail

down a specific time, the person may feel like you are blowing them off, so if you do need to meet them, schedule a time to meet or call.

Training Others in Your Life

Another thing that bothers me is the notion that we must get it all done because 'it' (whatever that may be) is our job. My home is fairly traditional; there are 'pink' jobs and 'blue' jobs. If I don't do the pink jobs—who will? There are almost unwritten rules in a lot of traditional households about who does what, especially if it has never been discussed before. I find people just fall into patterns. If you don't do something, one of two things happen:

a) *It won't get done.* (And ask does it really matter? And if so, which ones should I absolutely do?)

b) *The other people in your life might do it.* The danger is in thinking, or getting others to think (or trained to think), that certain things are our job. To illustrate this point I wanted to share some examples from friends of mine who leave their husbands and kids for a period of time. Within the first few days, women have told me that their husbands phone them and these are some of the questions (and complaints) they get:

i) Blaming her for things not done, like cleaning out the fridge before she left and eating something without checking the date first.

ii) Wondering how to use the washing machine, or better yet, where is the laundry soap? Guess where it was—beside the washing machine!

iii) Finding out how to fill out a form for a school trip for one of the kids.

iv) No milk left.

I guess in my discussions with women, I ask, "How come they call? How come they don't know? Have they never done this before? Have they always relied on their significant other or someone else to do this?" My only guess is that someone else has always done it, so why would it be their job now?

While trying to build our careers (whether on a volunteer or paid basis), taking on more responsibility outside of the home we do stretch ourselves thin. The frustrations set in and then we usually do not succeed in any area, leaving us feeling guilt, shame and all those other negative emotions.

To fix this dilemma we can not only use standard relaxation and stress management techniques (which, by the way, do work), but also look for ways to get things off our list completely. **Don't Get it All Done! Get Help!** Use the delegation skills taught in this book at work and at home. Just as you would develop or teach people at work, teach people in your life what you need done.

My husband (who is amazingly helpful in so many ways) even does his own laundry now. He is completely responsible for when he needs his clothes and uniforms for work and we no longer fight over it. It took some negotiation and some discussion, but he is now happy, gets it when he needs it and folded the way he likes. He even knows where his underwear is at all times.

Velvet Hammers know we'll never get it all done; there is always something to do. You will need to take time out sometimes and simply not do it. I'm still practicing this one myself, and I'm getting better at it. I hope you find balance and when things get crazy, that you have a support network. If you don't, I hope you seek a support network, full of positive people that can keep you move forward. Remember, women are amazing at this, it might just be that science is on our side.

FINAL WORDS

Since you have got this far, I trust that you have enjoyed the book. My only hope is that you can continue to learn and build upon whatever wisdom or key learnings you've taken from this information. Learning should be lifelong; it keeps the brain strong, and so I encourage you to keep learning. If something is not working for you, try another tactic or strategy. Find a mentor or someone who you think handles things with grace and eloquence and gets things done. There are so many areas to cover in leadership and so many amazing resources for you.

There may be born leaders, but I know many more who were grown, supported and educated. I know golfing is not the only way to get a voice or to get ahead. It is a great game, though, and perhaps you already enjoy it. Having the opportunity to lead can be a great challenge and also a great reward. My greatest wish for you is that you have not only the skills to do well, **but the opportunity to make a difference!**

GREAT RESOURCES AND LINKS

GREAT WEBSITE ON BRAINS AND DIFFERENCES

Science and Nature
http://www.bbc.co.uk/science/humanbody/sex/index_coo
kie.shtml

WOMEN'S ORGANIZATIONS, RESOURCES AND WEBSITES

National Women's Business Council
www.nwbc.gov

Women's Radio
www.womensradio.com

Women's Calendar
www.womenscalendar.org

Pink Magazine
www.pinkmagazine.com

Women's Enterprise
www.women's-enterprise.com

eWomen Network
www.eWomennetwork.com

eWomen Publishing
www.eWomenPublishing.com

Executive Women's Golf Association
www.ewga.com

Business Women's Network
www.bwni.com

Center for Women's Business Research
www.nfwbo.org

Downtown Women's Club
www.downtownwomensclub.com

Catalyst
www.catalystwomen.org

Forum for Women Entrepreneurs and Executives
www.fwe.org

National Association of Female Executives
www.nafe.com

National Association of Women Business Owners
www.nawbo.org

Women's Business Enterprise National Council
www.wbenc.org

Women Impacting Public Policy
www.wipp.org

Women Presidents' Organization
www.womenpresidentsorg.com

4591114119

GREAT BOOKS

Moir, Anne Ph.D. and David Jessel, *Brain Sex: The Real Difference Between Men & Women.* Dell Books, 1991.

Barletta, Martha, *Marketing to Women: How to Understand, Reach, and Increase Your Share of the World's Largest Market Segment.* Dearborn, 2003.

Wilson, Marie C., *Closing the Leadership Gap: Why Women Can and Must Help Run the World.* Viking, 2004.

Wachs, Esther, *Why the Best Man for the Job is a Woman: The Unique Female Qualities of Leadership.* First Harper Collins Business, 2001.

Fisher, Helen, *The First Sex: The Natural Talents of Women and How They Are Changing the World.* The Ballantine Publishing Group, 1999.

Gray, John, Ph.D., *Men Are From Mars, Women Are From Venus.* Harper Collins, 1992.

ELAINE ALLISON is an international professional speaker, a wife and a mother. She has enthralled audiences from coast to coast in both the United States and Canada with her lively presentations and affable style. She is a particular favorite at women's conferences.

As one of Canada's first female prison guards in an all-male maximum security correctional facility at the age of nineteen, Elaine had a crash course in understanding how men and women interact with each other and lead people. Her life virtually depended on it! She began to truly observe how women dealt with conflict, leadership and power, themes she has built into *The Velvet Hammer: PowHERful Leadership Lessons for Women Who Don't Golf.*

In addition to her early career, Elaine has taught children with behavioral problems in a special education program, managed over 1400 unionized flight attendants (handling issues at 35,000 ft. while in the airline industry), and successfully handled the day to day challenges of various large corporations as a manager (and then as a senior executive) for a technology firm. She learned how damaging some behaviors and choices can be, and with this book, has provided answers.

As a contributing author to *Speak Up, Speak Out,* this international speaker and author is determined to make a difference in the lives of women leaders, managers and supervisors around the world.

Elaine has also won the *2002 Visions of Excellence, Entrepreneur of the Year Award* for her speaking and consulting business.

I believe women have an amazing opportunity to contribute to our corporations, politics, associations and organizations around the world. For many years we have made great strides, and continue to make advances in many areas. I have a personal goal, and that is to help as many women as possible rise in the ranks of leadership, where I know they will make remarkable contributions. With ready skills in hand, women can make a difference.

If you know a Friend, Sister, Mother, Daughter, Aunt or anyone who would benefit from this information, feel free to recommend this book or you might want to purchase it as a gift.

Feel free to visit
The Velvet Hammer Portal
www.thevelvethammer.com
where you will find:

Additional resources such as:

- Training CDs
- Articles
- Evaluations
- Checklists
- Other sources for information and website links (updated as they become available)
- Gifts such as:
  —**Velvet Hammer** line of jewelry for the woman who gets a promotion or needs to be recognized (simply elegant and unique)

— Velvet Hammer "I've survived another day of leadership" oversized night shirts to give you support after a long day

Other *Velvet Hammer* Books Coming Soon:

The Velvet Hammer Negotiates a Raise and Everything Else She Wants

The Velvet Hammer Starts Her Own Business

SPEAKING ENGAGEMENTS

If you would like Elaine to speak at an upcoming event, please call toll-free at 1-866-241-6876 to check availability.

For a list of keynotes, training and workshops, visit:

www.elaineallison.com

Created especially for you...

To order extra copies for your organization or association; or if you know someone who would benefit from this book, order **on-line at:**

www.thevelvethammer.com

by phone or fax: Toll-Free: 1-866-241-6876

Please have the following information ready if calling;
(or print clearly if faxing)

NAME: (Last)_____(First)_____

ADDRESS:_____

CITY: _____, State/Province:_____

TELEPHONE: area code_____ _____

EMAIL ADDRESS: _____

_____

CREDIT CARD: ❐ VISA or ❐ MasterCard *(check one)*

CREDIT CARD # _____

EXPIRY DATE: _____

SIGNATURE: _____

Please send me _____ copies of *The Velvet Hammer: PowHERful Leadership Lessons for Women Who Don't Golf*

Bulk discounts available; please contact us for a quote.

Amount   _____$19.95 US
Enclosed: _____$24.95 CDN (PLUS 7% GST)
             _____ Shipping $4.00 US / $5.00 CDN
             _____ TOTAL

BY MAIL (with check payable to):   *We make every effort to*
Positive Presentations Plus Inc.   *ship immediately; in some*
2241 Stafford Ave.   *cases please allow 4-6*
Port Coquitlam, BC V3C 4X5   *weeks for delivery.*